Street Negotiation

How to Resolve Any

Conflict Anytime

Street Negotiation

How to Resolve Any

Conflict Anytime

Tristan J. Loo

All rights reserved. No part of this publication may be reproduced, stored in a retrieval system, or transmitted in any form or by any means—electronic, mechanical, photocopy, recording, or any other—except for brief quotations in printed reviews, without the prior permission of the publisher.

Copyright © 2006

ISBN: 1-58961-435-6
Published by PageFree Publishing, Inc.
109 South Farmer Street
Otsego, MI 49078
(269) 692-3926
www.pagefreepublishing.com

Dedicated to my loving parents
Margaret and Longden Loo
Who have stood by my side
Through good times and bad
And made me the person I am today.
Thank you for believing in me.

To be successful, it's not enough to know what you want in life. You have to know what it will take to get you there, what you have to sacrifice to get it, and most of all, you have to love it enough to be able to persevere during the hardest times.

~Tristan J. Loo

Acknowledgments

Most projects in life are not possible by one person alone. This book represents an investment of time and dedication from the many people that have supported me throughout its completion.

First and foremost, I would like to thank my parents, *Margaret & Longden Loo,* for their support in keeping me motivated to complete this project. Their dedication towards seeing this book reach completion was at times more obstinate than my own.

And to those who have always stood by me, my warmest thanks to my family members who have inspired me with their own lives: *Dyani, Kelsy, & Tomo Loo, Rosie Takagi, Max, Nomel, Taylr, and Beau Takagi, Lily Loo and the late Stanely Loo, Henry & Linda Loo, Brian Loo, Jennifer Loo, Kelley Low, and Tiffany Loo, Cecilia & Tak Wong, Kristopher, Jason, & Randall Wong, Lynne Minami-Johnson, Arlene & Wayne Minami, and Mary Okamoto.*

Many thanks to my good friend *Num Kutz* for watching my back through all the many years we've known each other. We've both experienced some rather turbulent times in our lives, but I've always appreciated the fact that when times got tough, he was one of the few who stayed by my side.

My inspiration for success has always come from my good friend *Randy Crowson.* Randy showed me, through his own achievements, that no dream is impossible if you possess the drive and dedication to reach it. Besides being a loyal friend, I don't think I personally know of any one else who has patented his own technology, and paved new ground in an industry before. Randy has been my Zen master of business wisdom.

Um agradecimento especial a *Estela Slomp Romand* por me mostrar que as pessoas podem ser confiáveis neste mundo. Obrigado por me dar força para me reerguer e enfrentar as fases mais difíceis. Sempre te amarei. *"Lamb-in-the-land."*

My deepest gratitude to my good friends for lending me their ideas and helping me throughout this project. I could not have finished this project without them. So with that in mind, thanks to: *Haady Lashkari, Christine*

Mabesa, *Ruben Ruckman, Mike Kelley, Nicole Longnecker, Eric Smutko, Jason Inouye, Trevor Metz, Yoko Nakai, Eli Dunlap, Serena Argil, Donald Mahr, Lygia Bortoloti, Danny Bahamondes, Loretta Tse, Mark Grider, Tanise Vargas, Wendy Vertiz, Aline Gaeta, Brian Davies, Veronica Caballero, Diana Slomp, Eda Slomp, Jacquelyne Ta, Patricia Araujo, Bruna Delvalle, and Jana Grael Farias* for being great friends.

Thanks also to *Aneeta Mitha* for her generous contribution in writing the foreword for my book.

Every student needs a master to guide them and to mold them into a person of character. I consider the following people to be the masters who have shown me the path towards enlightenment: *Coach Mircea Badulescu, Coach Matt Purkiss, John Turner, Jim Beautrow, Darrick Brunk, Tom Higgins, Jim Brittle, and Alton Brown.*

Finally, a heartfelt thanks and salute to all those *street cops* out there who risk their lives everyday out on the tough streets of our cities to keep us safe. You know the importance of Street Negotiation and I wrote this book with you in mind. Stay safe.

Special Thanks To the Following Professionals:

Consulting by Randy Crowson, President, Crowson Technologies
www.crowsontech.com

Cover design by Mike Bennett Graphics
www.mikebennettgraphics.com

Editing by Judith A. Habert
www.writeondemand.com

Contents

Acknowledgments viii
Foreword 1
Introduction 3

Part I: Arming Yourself with Negotiating Skills

1 The Art of Negotiating 9

What's a Negotiation? 9
What's the Difference Between a Negotiation, Mediation, and Arbitration? 10
A Brief History on Interest-Based Negotiating 12
The Goal of Interest-Based Negotiating 12
Why Do Most People Take Up Positional Bargaining? 13
Empty Your Cup 14
Barriers to a Successful Negotiation 15
The Three Ingredients of Street Negotiation 15
No Superior Styles, Only Superior Minds 16
The Four Types of Negotiating Outcomes? 17
Walking On Water 19
The Six Steps to Turn Conflict Into Agreement—PERPOS ... 20

2 Dealing With Difficult People 23

What Defines a Difficult Person? 23
General Rules for Difficult People 24
The Intimidator 25
Without Fear 26
Techniques for the Intimidator 26
The Manipulator 27

Identifying a Manipulator..28
Can I Negotiate With a Manipulator? 28
The Complainer...29
Techniques for the Complainer...29
The Gossiper..30
Techniques for the Gossiper 31
The Back-Stabber..34
Techniques for the Back-Stabber..35
The Bureaucrat 37
Techniques for the Bureaucrat 38

3 Secrets of Nonverbal Communication 41

What's Proxemics?..42
Why is Proxemics Important for a Negotiation? 43
What is our Comfort Zone?...43
Avoid Violating Personal Space 44
Proximity Separates the Strong from the Weak...........................44
Are They Using Barriers?...45
Using Proxemics for Emotional Emphasis...................................45
Where Should I Sit?..46
The Tea Combat..47
Physical Appearance 48
The First Impression before the First Impression.......................48
How to Improve Your 5-Second First Impression 49
What Message Does Your Body-Type Convey To Others?.......50
What Does Your Hair Say About You? 51
What You Wear Is Important..52
Color Cues..54
What Does the Face Say? 54
Smiling..55
Facial Expressions 55
Eye Contact and Eye Movement 56
Interpreting Eye Movements and Eye Contact...........................56
Gain Rapport by Maintaining Eye Contact..................................57
Eye Movement and Deception 58

Body Language 59
Posture and Stance 59
Gestures 60
Head Gestures 61
Torso Gestures 61
Arm Gestures 61
Hand Gestures 62
Leg/Foot Gestures 63
Other Gestures 63
How to Say More Than Words 64
Interpreting Paralanguage 64
Using Paralanguage to Your Advantage 65
A Touch Can Mean A Thousand Words 66
Categories of Touch 67
Tips on Communicative Touch 68
How to Send the Right Messages With a Handshake 69
Cultural Differences 70

4 Establishing Rapport, Building Trust 71

What is Trust? 72
The 15 Ingredients to Build a Trusted Relationship 72
Mirroring to Gain Rapport 75
How Do You Know When You Have Established Rapport? .. 76
Other Factors in Rapport-Building 77
Important Trust-Building Strategies 78
Is that So? 81
How Do I Gain Forgiveness From Another? 82
Deception Comes Back to Bite You 83
The Promised Picnic 84
The Nature of Things 84
Effective Praising 85
General versus Specific Praise 86
How to Give Effective Praise 88
How to Give Criticism Without Bruising Egos 88

Part II: How to Defuse Anger and Reach Agreements in 6 Easy Steps

Step I
Plan Ahead 92

Develop a Back-up Plan 93
The Hostage Negotiator's Alternative...........................94
Advantages of Having a Back-up Plan 94
The Stone Cutter...95
Empowering Your Alternative 96
Let Your Plan B Tell You Whether or Not You Should
    Negotiate..97
Keep Your Back-Up Plan Confidential.........................98
Be Able To Walk Away From the Negotiating Table 99
Establish Your Bottom Line..99
Anticipate Your Counterpart's Alternatives 100
How to Uncover Your Interests—and Theirs 100
Positional Versus Interest-Based Negotiating.............101
Why Positional Negotiating Creates Problems...........102
Discover Your Interests underneath Your Positions ..103
Identify Possible Options..104
Consider Fair Standards 104
Identify the Other Side's Interests 104
What Kind of Negotiating Power Do You Have?......105
Positional Powers..105
Acquired Powers...107
Destiny...108
Befriend Time 108
Deadlines 109
Gain Negotiating Leverage through Intelligence-Gathering..110
Know Your Opponent before Stepping Into the Ring..........110
Know Exactly with who you Should be Negotiating With 111
Other Topics to Research..112
Where Should you Conduct your Negotiation? 114
Types of Communication Options 114
Creative Alternatives to Office-Based Meetings........116

Some Advice on Using Telephones 116

Step II Emotional Control 119

Worse Than a Clown 119
What Causes Anger? 120
Why Do We Really Care What They Say? 121
What is Egotism? 121
Why We Need to Control Anger 121
Self-Control 122
Sources of Anger 122
True Self 123
Additional Internal Contributors to Anger 123
Recognizing the Signs and Symptoms of Anger 124
Am I Right To Be Angry? 125
Factors That Lower Our Frustration Tolerance 125
The Spider 126
Rational Mind versus Emotional Mind 126
React = Lose 128
Three Ways We React 128
Tactical Withdrawal and Regroup 130
Apply H.E.A.T. When Tactical Withdrawal Is Not an Option 130
Be Careful Not to Label 132
Recognizing and Accepting the Facts Of Life 133
Assertiveness Is Not Always the Best Substitute for
    Aggression 133
The Eight-Worldly Winds 134
Stress Management 135
The Present Moment 135
What Is Stress? 135
Symptoms of Stress 136
Chronic Stress 138
What Are The Three Stages Of Stress? 138
Relaxation Techniques to Reduce Stress 138
Other Creative Stress-Reducing Techniques 140
Preventative Stress Maintenance 141

Step III Reduce Tension 143

Nothing Exists 143
Reduce Tension with Active Listening 144
Why Actively Listen? 144
Keeping Silent 145
What Are Burning Issues? 145
The Importance of Active Listening During a Negotiation ..145
The Four Steps to Active Listening 146
Listening and Understanding 148
Empathize to Gain Perspective 150
Strategies for Using Empathy 152
Asking Questions and Encouraging Communication 153
Paraphrasing 156
Dealing with Personal Attacks 158
Gift of Insults 158

Step IV Persuade 165

The Arguing Monks 165
Their Way versus Your Way 166
There's No Magic Behind Persuasion 167
Unlocking Them from Their Positions 167
Ask Questions to Uncover Interests 169
The Proud Archer 173
Persuasion Tactics 174
Counter-Tactics for Unfair Tactics 183
Setting Ground Rules 190

Step V Options 193

How to Invent Options 194
#1 Important Step for Creating Options 195
Brainstorm Cooperatively 195
Techniques on Dividing Property 196
Expanding the Pie 197

Who Makes The First Offer? 200
Carrying and Leaving 200
Using Fair Standards 201
Steps to Using Fair Standards 201
Types of Fair Standards 203
Mediation as a Solution to a Deadlock 203

Step VI Solutions 205

Reaching an Agreement 205
Barriers to Gaining Commitment 206
Don't Push, Guide Them 207
Don't Feed Them Your Ideas, Let Them Feel Like you Both Created it 208
Offer Possible Solutions and Let Them Criticize Them 208
Get it in Writing 208
Turning Options into Solutions 210
Cold Feet 210
Building a Dispute Resolution Plan into the Agreement 211
No Agreement? Use Your Plan B 211
Before You Walk Away From The Table 212
Executing your Back-Up Plan 212

Final Word 214
Street Glossary 215
References 223
About The Author, Tristan J. Loo 225
About Alternative Conflict Resolution Services 226

Foreword
By Aneeta K. Mitha

On any given day, people are faced with numerous confrontations that they must decide and act upon. If that is not enough, the people in our lives—our employers, family members, significant others, and strangers all crave some spotlight in our daily lives. Though these confrontations may be unavoidable, the transformation from confrontation to conflict can be avoided. These external tensions are derived from our internal conflicts—self-esteem, self-preservation, and past experiences. Such conflicts within us dictate how well we act with others and how we respond to situations that take place.

The fear of inadequacy is embedded in our minds from birth until death. This fear arises from the unreasonable expectations that the media places on society. With ridiculous standards of beauty, wealth, and social status, a distorted mindset takes shape and replaces the once content and self-valued way of thinking. When faced with confrontation, we become disabled from creating a tactful and intelligent response to deal with it. After such a response is put into action, we become unable to stand firm with our beliefs. With each failed confrontation, insecurities deepen and it then becomes inevitable: it is no longer a confrontation—what we are now faced with is pure conflict.

In life there are always the paired opposites: black and white, up and down, and the self-loather and the self-preserver. As one part of the population gets drawn into the absurdities of the media, the other part decides to ignore and to conquer—confrontations become war. Through means of aggression, this part of society begins to demean the opposing side's value and status, which in turn increases its own. With each victory, the self-preserver further retaliates in a brutal and relentless battle, which of course, the self-loather is ill equipped to defeat. And so this pattern will continue. Truth be said, a life of war is a life of unhappiness, full of enemies and eventual self-hatred.

There is one division of society that is minimally seduced by the media and is potent enough to virtually go untouched by aggression—the gray area of society. This area, which could encompass the other two parts of society as well, is the area populated by the haunted—troubled by the past. The loss of a loved one through relocation, break up, or death can result in our need to detach. When such a process occurs, confrontations become events to be avoided—we take flight from the situation or the opposing person entirely. These confrontations transform into internal conflicts, which then become ingrained into our minds. As each confrontation is left without closure, they build up and begin to alter our personality.

When one of these three scenarios are enacted, situations that were once confrontations soon become conflicts that are much deeper than we can imagine. Acquiring a healthy sense of self is the key step in dealing with confrontations successfully because all three have the same underlying problem—a contorted version of self-worth. As our self-esteem becomes stronger, so too does our means of problem solving. No longer do we need to give up our beliefs, belittle others, or run at the sight of confrontation—rational thought and confidence will prevail.

As one of the leading experts in practical peacemaking and negotiation, Mr. Loo has distilled the essence of conflict resolution into a purposeful guide designed for the average individual. Mr. Loo has seen the horrors that destructive conflict can bring to society and he also knows that conflict is an unavoidable part of everyone's life. The strategies he has presented in this book document his knowledge and commitment in dealing with personal conflict through the use of fairness and integrity. *Street Negotiation* is something that everyone can use in their lives.

Aneeta K. Mitha
Author/Peacemaker
San Diego, CA
November 30, 2005

Introduction

We negotiate to some degree on a daily basis with everyone we meet. You probably never even realized that you've been using negotiation tactics since the day you were an infant. You see, *negotiation is about resolving conflicts* and conflicts arise everywhere—in the workplace, at the home, at a restaurant, even out on the street. Conflicts come about when two parties have opposing views, positions, needs and interests and are unwilling to see things differently. Conflicts can be as trivial as two people fighting over a parking spot, or it can be as serious as a terrorist with a bomb in a school bus. To successfully resolve conflict, you need to have a framework to follow. That framework is called *Street Negotiation* because its main application is to help you with your daily personal life as well as your professional one, through effective communication skills and by understanding some basic rules of human behavior.

What is Street Negotiation?

Street Negotiation is a process that you can use to deal with most situations where the other side doesn't see things the same as you do. Street Negotiation is not about winning or losing. Its about reaching agreements over what is fair and preserving important long-term relationships.

Why learn to Negotiate?

Street Negotiation is not only a professional tool, it's also a life skill that's equally as effective in your personal life as it is in your professional one. Conflict happens whenever two people have differing views and ideas on a problem that they both share. The same skills you will learn to negotiate with a business partner can work equally as well on a spouse, friend, or family member. *Street Negotiation* allows you to solve the problem cooperatively by first dealing with the emotions involved and then focusing on the process of communication, rather than on the issues of right versus wrong, or force against force.

Some of the people who can benefit from this book:

- Law enforcement officials
- Teachers
- Social workers
- Managers & supervisors
- Employees
- Business professionals
- Customer service employees
- Husbands & Wives
- Parents
- Members of the clergy
- Mediators
- National leaders
- And anyone else who wants to benefit from reaching an agreement without fighting.

What can Street Negotiation Teach You?

The purpose of *Street Negotiation* is to give you the know-how to *effectively communicate with any person you encounter*, whether it is at work or at home. Street Negotiation gives you the tools you need to set you on the path for becoming a master at reaching agreements.

In this book you will learn how to:

- Gain the upper-hand in any negotiation with preparation
- Deal with the most difficult personalities
- Read and speak nonverbal communication
- Gain rapport and build trust
- Control you anger—*and theirs*
- Communicate better through active listening
- Reframe verbal attacks away from you
- Make your enemy into your partner
- Get the other side to cooperate in generating mutually-satisfying solutions

How to Use This Book

I wrote this book especially for the average person out there who wants to learn the techniques of conflict resolution, effective communication and negotiating skills. *Street Negotiation* breaks each phase of the negotiating process down into *easy* to follow steps. It is designed to be used out there on the *street*, so it's written in a way that *anyone* can follow.

By applying the techniques described in this book, you will develop the foundation to be able to successfully negotiate conflicts, big and small, and also help you realize how powerful and beneficial effective communication can be for your daily life out there on the street.

What's With the Zen Stories?

A Zen story is short and witty story that has a very powerful message built into it. The purpose of the Zen stories in this book is not a religious one, but rather to highlight the importance of a certain chapter or technique within this book. Zen stories are effective because they don't give the answer away. They engage the reader and force them to look inward and discover the true meaning of the stories for themselves. Both the teachings of Zen and martial arts are designed to be simple. They take the essence of the teaching and whittle away the parts that are not needed until they have just the basic naked form of the technique. So many other books and teachings cloud the mind with useless information, so the goal with *Street Negotiation* is to tackle conflict resolution in a *Zen-like approach* and take all the negotiating techniques out there and distill them into their most basic forms.

The Zen stories in this book are designated by an italicized header and text font. I'm sure you will find these stories both educational and enlightening.

Part I
Arming Yourself with Negotiating Skills

A young bird who understands how to fly will still fall without feathers.

~Tristan Loo

1
The Art of Negotiating

Empty your mind, be formless. Shapeless, like water. Now you put water into a cup, it becomes the cup. You put water into a bottle it becomes the bottle. You put it into a teapot it becomes the teapot. Now, water can flow, or it can crash. Be water my friend...

~Lee Jun Fan (Bruce Lee)

What's A Negotiation?

What comes to mind when I mention the word negotiation? Buying a car or house? Closing a business deal? Talking a hostage-taker into giving up his hostages? How often do you think you negotiate on a daily basis? Well, when you really think about it, *we negotiate constantly throughout our normal everyday lives.* We negotiate with the car mechanic on the price of his services and when the car will be available. We negotiate with our spouse on what to eat for dinner. We negotiate with our children on when they should go to bed. Heck, we even negotiate with our pet dog to stay out of the trash. A negotiation is a discussion between two or more people with the purpose of reaching an agreement that is better than what they could have achieved without negotiating. Why then if we use negotiation skills everyday, do we consider the word *negotiation* with some sort of curiosity as if it were a special power that is out of our grasp? Its because we are taught early on to say the wrong things to gain the compliance of others. We react rather than respond, and tend to damage relations rather than restore balance. We allow our emotions to control our mouths, rather than our minds. All this works against facilitating cooperation, which is one of the guiding principles in the philosophy of Street Negotiation. Learning how to negotiate, how to resolve conflict, and how to gain voluntary compliance is a life skill that should be practiced everyday.

What's the Difference Between a Negotiation, Mediation, and Arbitration?

It's important that we clarify the difference between these terms to avoid confusion in the future. Negotiation, mediation, and arbitration are all forms of conflict resolution; however, there are differences among them.

Negotiation. Involves two or more parties who are engaged in direct discussions to reach an agreement. Both parties use persuasion and influence to get the other side to agree with them.

   Example:

- A buyer and a salesman are negotiating a price for a car.
- A wife is negotiating with her husband over use of finances.
- A president is negotiating with another country's leader to remove intercontinental ballistic missile silos that threaten the security of the nation.

Mediation. Similar to negotiation, but mediation involves the use of a neutral third-party who assists the negotiating parties in reaching an agreement. Mediation is used typically when direct negotiations have failed because the mediator can separate the people from the problem much easier than the stakeholders can.

<u>Example</u>

- A buyer purchases a used car from a seller. The car breaks down soon after. The buyer demands his money back. The seller accuses the buyer of damaging the car himself. Both parties decide to handle the situation out of court with the help of a neutral third-party.
- A couple decide to get a divorce, but argue over who gets what. Instead of paying for their own lawyers and legal services, they decide to work out their agreement with a training divorce mediator. The mediator uncovers what the needs and interests are for both parties, instead of focusing in on their positions and demands, thus paving the way for agreement.
- Two nations, on the verge of war after failed negotiations, agree to peace-talks. Neither side trusts the other side, so they ask for the help of a neutral country to act as mediator for their talks. Through the mediator, both stake-holding countries are able to work out an agreement.

Arbitration. Arbitration is similar to mediation in that an objective third party is used, however, the main difference is that instead of helping the parties reach their own agreement, the arbitrator listens to both sides and then passes judgment on a winner and a loser.

<u>Example:</u>

- Two employees are having issues with each other. They take these issues to the boss. The boss hears both sides and then decides to fire one of the employees.
- Two siblings are having a fight and the mother gets involved. The

mother hears what they have to say, and of course both siblings are pointing fingers at the other side. The mother decides to ground them both.

A Brief History on Interest-Based Negotiating

During the 1970s the Harvard Negotiation Project, spearheaded by William Ury and Roger Fisher, sought to answer the question, "What is the best way for people to deal with their differences?" Through their research, Ury and Fisher discovered that the traditional model of bargaining was both inefficient and unnecessarily hostile to both parties. They realized that the best way to facilitate an agreement was not through positional bargaining, but rather through mutual understanding of interests and cooperative brainstorming. This discovery led to their 1981 best-selling book, *Getting to Yes*. In the book, the Harvard experts argue for a concept known now as principled negotiation, or win-win negotiating. Instead of competing against one-another for concessions, the principled negotiation strategy sought to work together as a team to solve the problem together while preserving the relationship. The goal of principled negotiating was being hard on the problem, while at the same time being soft on the person.

The Goal of Interest-Based Negotiating

A lot of people liken the negotiating game to a strategic competition such as chess—one person trying to obtain a tactical advantage over the other person. The problem with this approach is inevitably it leaves someone as a winner and someone as a loser. When we take psychology into account, this type of negotiating mindset leaves us with broken feelings and resentment, neither of which is good for reputation or renegotiation. We negotiate on a daily basis and 80% of the people that we deal with we are going to deal with again at some point in time. Having a win-lose mentality while negotiating might get you what you want now, but in the long run, it will ruin relationships and create conflict and resentment in your life.

The goal in any type of conflict resolution should be mutual satisfaction, rather than trying to get more and make fewer concessions than the other side. You want to win the person over rather than winning over him. Other written material on negotiations refers to the other party as opponent, adversary, or even enemy. This is not the case with Street Negotiation. The person is not your opponent, but rather your counterpart or partner. You and your negotiating partner are a team working on solving a complex problem with creative options that will fit the needs that both of you have. This point of Street Negotiation should be made clear—the goal is not to win, but rather to reach an agreement with the other side that is based on what is fair, not on who is right, more powerful, or more deceptive.

Why Do Most People Take Up Positional Bargaining?

Positional bargaining is what we think of when we go to the flea market. One guy makes an offer and the other guy tries to make the first guy come up or down from that initial offer, depending if they are the buyer or seller. Posititional bargaining is simple and easy to do. It requires little thought, no preparation, and no emotional control to carry out. Positional bargaining is great for things that do not require much time or effort, such as buying a used chair at a swap meet, because our time is valued as more precious than the chair is worth and therefore positional negotiating is a simple and efficient means of exchange. It can even be made into a formula—your attached value on the item, over the amount money you are willing to spend, versus the sellers interest in your money over the item they have to sell, simple right? Sure, but when the negotiations become more complex, such as interpersonal disputes and relationship negotiating, then those positional bargaining formulas don't work very well. Street Negotiation focuses on handling complex or emotional conflicts rather than positional ones because if we use positional bargaining in high stakes games such as relationships, then we tend to make stupid and needless bargaining mistakes, such as the number of unnecessary divorces that occur every year just because one side threatens the other side with a position (divorce) and the other side calls their bluff, locking both parties to an ultimate fate of divorce that both sides never really wanted in the first place.

Empty Your Cup

A well-known professor at the university asked a Zen master if they could have tea one afternoon so that the professor could learn more about Zen from the master. The two sat down at the table and the professor began to talk lavishly about everything he knew of Zen while the master was serving the tea. As he was giving his speech, the professor noticed that his tea cup was full, but that the Zen master was continuing to pour tea into the cup, spilling the tea onto the table. Finally, this annoyed the professor so much that he interrupted his speech and blurted out, "Stop! Can't you see that the cup is full already?"

The master smiled at the professor and said, "But you asked to learn about Zen? How can I teach you anything if your cup is already full?"

We are not given any formal education early in life how to negotiate with others, except for maybe a few pieces of good advice from our parents. We learn these skills by imitating other people and holding onto the tactics that work best for us. In time, we become like the professor in this story by filling our minds with preconceptions of what is the best way of resolving conflict and reaching agreements. But in order to become a master at dealing with others, you must first empty your cup and become receptive to new ideas and new ways of handling people problems.

Barriers to a Successful Negotiation

A negotiation takes place anytime you discuss your ideas with another person with the intent of getting them to see the situation your way. However, when the other party does not want to accept your ideas, three conflict-generating actions can take place on their part:

- They *dig into* their own position and aggressively *defend* it.
- They *attack your ideas* in an attempt to weaken them.
- They will *attack you* personally.

All of us resolve conflict everyday without even realizing that we are negotiating, but often we adopt a positional style of negotiating where we make a demand without keeping our minds open to other options that might satisfy our needs. While haggling over demands is simple—it also creates an environment that breeds conflict. What we therefore need is a way of resolving conflict where the needs of each party are discussed before any solution is created.

Street Negotiation is not only a way to persuade others through effective communication, but it's also a system by which you can resolve everyday conflicts and at the same time prevent yourself from being a victim of verbal abuse.

The Three Ingredients of Street Negotiation

Every expert has their own opinion on the key ingredients of their style of negotiation. As a martial arts fighter and a student of Zen philosophy, I liken the art of negotiation to that of being a skillful fighter. Therefore, in its most basic element, Street Negotiation is made up of three elements: Flexibility, Respect, and Cooperation.

Flexibility—be like the nature of water. Negotiating is a dynamic process—things change, people react, and nothing ever remains the same. In any type of negotiation, your flexibility or your ability to adapt to unexpected changes becomes your greatest power. Bruce Lee once said that in order to overcome your adversary, you must be like the nature of water because it can trickle gently or crash with tremendous force. It can conform to the shape of any container and yet be formless at the same time. Water cannot be hurt and it offers no target to be punched or attacked. Adopt this as your negotiation philosophy. *Be like water* when you negotiate and be able to conform to any situation and avoid attacks by offering no target for them to attack. Be able to conform to the shape of the situation to meet its particular needs.

Respect—the credo of the street. The second ingredient of Street Negotiation is *respect*. The one universal language that everyone understands is respect. Not everyone has everything they want in life, and many will never get what they want, but what they do expect is to be respected for who they are, no matter how bad or good they might be. Respect does not mean that you like the person or that you agree with them. Respect means that you treat them like you want to be treated yourself. Gang members and police officers are often bitter enemies, yet both understand the meaning of respect. An officer can make an arrest on a gang member, but still show respect to that gang member by treating him with dignity. Another officer can do the same job, but disrespect a gang member by embarrassing them or causing them to lose face in front of their peers, which could result in bitterness and resentment between them personally in the future, making that officer's job a lot more dangerous. Likewise, Street Negotiation is not about disrespecting people with deceptive tactics, lies, or shark-like strategies used by some aggressive negotiators because that would break the fundamental rule of the street. Whether you personally like them or not, you must always give your counterpart the respect that they deserve. This means you should always negotiate wearing your professional face and never make it personal.

Cooperation—becoming one with your adversary. The third principle of Street Negotiation is cooperation. Most people believe that a negotiation is a win-lose battle. They believe that if one person gains something, it means the other side has to give something up. This is however not always true. Street Negotiation is a way of dealing with everyone in your life—both professionally and personally, and by adopting the principle of cooperation into your negotiating style, you address the needs, interests, and emotions of the other side as well as your own. A poor negotiation is where one side wins and the other side loses. In a Street Negotiation, both sides walk away with their interests being met and also walk away satisfied because they have worked together to come up with a reasonable solution that was acceptable and fair to both parties. Think of your counterpart as your partner—not your enemy, and the real adversary is the problem that both of you face together.

No Superior Styles, Only Superior Minds

Just as there are many different styles of martial arts, there are different styles of negotiating. Just like martial arts, there will never cease to exist wild debates over which style is superior. This is because there is no answer to this debate. All styles of martial arts and negotiating are imperfect. As in the martial arts, negotiators will claim that their style is superior, but if this were true then there would not be many systems of negotiating out there today—each one exploits the weaknesses of the other style. Let me tell you that there is no one style of negotiating that is the best. What you must do is learn every style that you can and incorporate those aspects that work best for you.

Superiority lies not within the style, but within the person and their self knowledge. A proficient fighter will learn a style, master, make it part of his being and dissolve that knowledge within him. A master warrior does not lock himself into one style of combat, but rather masters many styles of fighting and picks the most useful techniques that work for his particular skills, build, and abilities. There are many different styles of negotiating and each one is geared at producing some level of results. There is no one particular style that is better than the other in producing results. It just depends on desired outcome that you wish to produce. Hard-styles of negotiating are aggressive and positional in nature, pitting force upon force. Deceptive negotiating uses tricks and false promises to gain an outcome that is favorable to you. Both will produce favorable results, but in return, the other side must suffer. Street Negotiation is not concerned with winning or losing, but rather getting what is fair, preserving relationships, and defusing anger and emotion.

The Four Types of Negotiating Outcomes?

Negotiating outcomes are the types of results that can happen at the end of a negotiation. All negotiations end up with one out of four possible outcomes: one party wins and the other loses, both parties lose, they get stuck in a stalemate, or both end up winning. Obviously, the goal in Street Negotiation is for both parties to walk away with their needs being satisfied. Familiarize yourself with the four different negotiating outcomes.

The lose-lose outcome. In this type of outcome, egos come into play which thwarts the negotiating process. Both sides dig into their positions and are unwilling to compromise with each other. In the end, both parties end up losing in the deal. Resentment exists between both parties as a result of the outcome and it is unlikely that they will ever negotiate with each other again.

<u>Example</u>

A labor union refuses a contract offer and goes on strike until demands are met. The company refuses to give into to this bullying-type technique and digs into their position of not budging. In the end, the strikers go back to work without a raise and with lost income and the company loses a large amount of sales revenue, and the consumer loses because the company must raise prices to pay for its losses.

The win-lose outcome. In this type of outcome, one side wins and the other side loses. There is no compromise with a win-lose outcome. It's a one-side takes all battle, with one side getting all their needs satisfied, and the other side getting nothing. While the side that wins may be very happy about the outcome; the losing side has a high level of resentment over the deal because they did not have any of their needs met. This usually results in an end to any future negotiations and a termination of the relationship.

<u>Examples</u>

A street brawl is the ultimate in win-lose negotiations. One side wins by use of physical violence and the losing side has no choice but to submit to defeat.

A civil court battle is win-lose. A judge or jury decides winner and loser based on available evidence. One side wins punitive or compensatory damages and the other side loses that money.

The stalemate. In this type of outcome, neither side wins or loses and after a long negotiating session, both sides are at the exact same place that they started off at. This is a result of not being able to deal with interests and only positions. Stalemates happen when both sides aggressively defend their positions and neither side is able to make the other side budge.

> Example
>
> You go to buy a car and the salesman quotes you a price that is too high. You are unwilling to budge on your price and the salesman is unwilling to budge on his quote. You then walk out of the dealership and go find another one to deal with and the salesman moves on to the next customer.

The win-win outcome. This is the type of outcome that you strive to achieve when you Street Negotiate. In this type of outcome, both sides walk away with their interests and needs being met. Both sides leave the negotiating table satisfied because they came out of the negotiation with more than they had started with. Relationships are preserved because both parties cooperated with each other in determining a fair solution to the problem. This outcome also bolsters trust for future negotiations between the two parties because they have established a positive relationship.

> Example
>
> Two neighbors want ownership of an apple tree on divided ground. Instead of taking up the position of owning or not owning the tree, both parties explore the reasons behind why they want ownership of the tree. Party A want to own it so that he can cut it down because the tree drops apples all over his lawn. Party B loves the tree for the sweet apples it produces. They come to an agreement that the tree can stay as long as Party B maintains the tree and collects all of its fruit. Both parties have their needs met.

Walking On Water

A well-known master was waiting at the foot of a lake for a ferry to take him to the other side. A monk approached the master and laughed at him, asking how come the master was so great if he could not walk on water. The monk removed his sandals and walked out on top of the water without sinking. He began to skip and dance on top of the water to mock the skill that the master lacked.

The master replied to the monk, "This is truly a miraculous skill that you possess. How long did it take you to learn this skill?"

"It took me 35 years of intense training to learn this skill....Yet, I am only a monk and you are a master. Why is this?"

The ferry pulled up to the shore and the master stepped aboard and paid his fare to the boat-master. As the boat began to push off shore, the master looked back at the monk who was still waiting for an answer, "Because it took me 10 minutes and one gold coin to do the same thing," the master replied.

The true art of negotiating is not about learning every single tactic and counter tactic in the book, but rather it adheres to a simple framework that can be used as the foundation to solve most conflict situations that arise. In conflict resolution, as with the martial arts, there is no particular right way of doing something, only a way that works for that situation. In that sense, it would be useless to teach you tactic and counter-tactic and expect that you memorize all of them in a real life setting. This would be like learning how to walk on water. Instead, Street Negotiation empowers you with the understandings of how people act, react, and deal, thereby, allowing you to choose the path towards an agreement.

The 6 Steps to A Successful Negotiation—PERPOS

No two negotiations will ever be the same. A negotiation is a highly dynamic process and it involves people with different backgrounds, levels of frustration, emotions, and objectives. The situation might be the same, but it will always be the people involved in the negotiation who will make it exciting and challenging. Although the personalities of the people will be different, there are certain techniques that will give you the upper-hand in any dispute. Learn these six steps, acronymed as PERPOS, and you will be able to resolve any type of negotiation or conflict that comes your way.

Plan ahead. Preparation is the key to boosting your negotiating power in any negotiation. You must create and develop your Plan B—your walk-away alternative to boost your negotiating power and to set parameters for your negotiating goals. Research and gain the power of knowledge on the person, company, product, or issue being negotiated.

Emotional control. Anger is your most dangerous opponent in a negotiation because it causes reaction to occur instead of rational and logical thought. Learn to respond positively and proactively to someone's verbal abuse rather than letting anger take control of your actions.

Reduce tension. Their anger will be an obstacle for you to overcome before you can even approach the problem because their emotions have taken control of their thought process. You must therefore use the tools of listening, asking, and paraphrasing, to safely vent away their anger and frustration. Fulfill their need to be heard and acknowledged. Collect information on their interests. Empathize with them to reduce tension and facilitate cooperative behavior from them. Reframe their personal attacks away from you and onto the problem instead.

Persuade. While you may be trying to reach an agreement, they might be trying to dominate you by making it a win-lose game. Don't play their game. Instead reframe competition into cooperation. Reframe the process of negotiating by focusing on their interests rather than positions. Concentrate on cooperative problem-solving rather than arguing.

Options. Learn how to create options from outside the box. Brainstorm options together as a team and subject those options through the filter of objective standards to generate a fair solution. Cooperate with each other in developing options that satisfy both of your interests.

Solutions. Those options then need to be agreed upon as being a solution to the conflict and put into action. If no agreement can be reached, then turn to your back-up plan as your alternative. Whether or not you reach an agreement, you will always be able to move forward with Street Negotiation.

2
Dealing with Difficult People

Who is right?
The first boy who thinks the dog is happy? Or the second boy who thinks the first boy does not truly know if the dog is happy? Or the third boy who thinks that the second boy does not truly know if the first boy does not know that the dog is happy or not?

~Chinese Proverb

What Defines A Difficult Person?

There is no one solid definition of a difficult person because there are numerous reasons why a person is difficult to begin with. Difficult behavior is simply that behavior which hinders the performance of others in completing their tasks. Difficult behavior in a person might be caused by their insecurity, their ability to only see a very narrow set of options, their confusion with mistaking assertiveness with aggression, or plainly they don't like you and they don't feel a desire to treat you with respect. No matter what type of difficult person you deal with, there are two things that remain the same: (1) they will try to get you to play their game and on their turf. (2) they will try to make you react rather than respond—two very different actions as we will discover later.

The Chinese zodiac is full of different animals, representing the different calendar years. We commonly associate with a certain animal based upon the year that we were born. These zodiac animals have associated traits with them that are supposed to be attributes that we also share if that is our assigned zodiac. Also these zodiac animals have certain affinities for some zodiacs, but dislikes for others. For example, the horse has the affinity for the tiger and the dog, but an enmity for the rat. The dragon has an affinity for the rat and the monkey, but an enmity for the dog. Like the Chinese zodiac, certain people will be more difficult to some rather than to others. This is why it is hard to classify people as difficult because what may be a difficult person to one might be an easy personality for another. Difficult people are traditionally comprised of several common classifications, and although each classification is not designed to be comprehensive of the complex psychological makeup of a person, it serves the purpose of setting some guidelines for you in how to deal with them effectively.

General Rules for Difficult People

When in doubt, try abiding by these four general rules for dealing with difficult people.

Don't play their game, change it. Whether they are intimidators, backstabbers, or manipulators, don't fall into the trap of playing their game because more often than not, they are better at it that you are. Also, by playing their game, you will be fighting an uphill battle because they will have the home-court advantage.

Don't give in, strategize. Just because they are difficult does not mean that they should get their way. Giving into a difficult person only serves to strengthen their behavior and leaves you feeling resentful. Pick your battles wisely. Know when to fight and when to retreat. Approach the situation tactically and consider all options prior to engagement.

Don't try to change the person, work on the behavior. You can't change a cat into a dog, or a horse into a duck. Don't make the same mistake of thinking that you can change a person into something they are not. Adopting the position that the person needs to change or can be changed will cause conflict. Instead, focus on the behavior that needs to be corrected.

Don't make their problem your problem. Difficult people want you to experience life as they do, so they use their tricks and tactics in order to bring you down to their level. Don't enter their world by taking their abuse personally. Instead, empathize with them and their position to gain a better understanding of who they are, but don't make their problem your problem

The Intimidator

Intimidators use aggressive-tactics and use fear as their primary strategy to get you to comply with their demands. Their overly aggressive style forces you to either defend or surrender to avoid the verbal abuse that you will suffer at their hands. The intimidator wants total control of the situation and gains that control by forcing you to hand over your own control to them through fear. The intimidator may use one of a combination of verbal abuse, yelling, nonverbal intimidation, and threats to get you to comply with their demands.

<u>An Intimidator is Characterized by:</u>

- Uses fear to coerce
- Aggressive tactics
- Controlling personality
- Demanding

- Threatening
- Egotistical
- Easily angered
- Self-centered
- Stubborn
- Possibly violent

Without Fear

During the civil wars in feudal Japan, an invading army would quickly sweep into a town and take control. In one particular village, everyone fled just before the army arrived - everyone except the Zen master. Curious about this old fellow, the general went to the temple to see for himself what kind of man this master was. When he wasn't treated with the deference and submissiveness to which he was accustomed, the general burst into anger. "You fool," he shouted as he reached for his sword, "don't you realize you are standing before a man who could run you through without blinking an eye!" But despite the threat, the master seemed unmoved. "And do you realize," the master replied calmly, "that you are standing before a man who can be run through without blinking an eye?"

Techniques for the Intimidator

Decide if it's worth your time. The intimidator uses verbal abuse to bait you into reacting with your emotional mind rather than responding with your rational one. Often they are not thinking with their rational minds either, so the environment for a successful negotiation might not even be there. Pick you battles wisely and know when to lose a battle in order to win the war. Sometimes it is best just to take a time-out and let everyone cool down before resuming with a negotiation. Time is on your side when dealing with the intimidator. They are the ones who want things to move quick.

Don't react to their aggression. The intimidator preys off of two emotions—fear and aggression. It's their advantage to get you to play on their field by eliciting either of these two reactions, so the first thing is not to play their game. Instead, change the game by focusing their attention away from you and onto the problem that you both face. Intimidators are comfortable in the YOU versus I environment. Change that environment to the US versus the PROBLEM playing field and their aggression will no longer work for them.

Acknowledge their power and move on. The intimidator wants you to play their power game because they are good at it and the problem that most people make is that they play the power game with the intimidator to which they often end up losing. Rather than compete with them, remove their incentive to put up a fight by acknowledging their power by telling them that they are right and apologize and then refocus the conversation back onto the problem. "You're right. I'm sorry. Let's work on this at another angle…" By doing this, you disarm the intimidator and tactically block their strategy of attacking you because there is no fight for them to win—you have told him that he's already won. This is an example of losing the battle to win the war.

The Manipulator

The manipulator is a very dangerous person to deal with because they prey on our emotional mind for their own selfish interests. The manipulator feeds your emotional need of self-esteem and acceptance in order to gain your cooperation in obtaining their own objectives. They create the illusion of trust, but in reality their interests are self-centered. Manipulators will make bold promises and ask you for cash in advance, but when it comes time to deliver, they are no where to be found. Manipulators are natural-born actors. Some are easy to spot, others you would never suspect. In my own life, I have experienced first hand the fact that a manipulator can ruin your life and leave you devastated without even blinking their eyes (…yeah, you know who you are), so take it from me—it can happen to the best of us. Negotiating with a manipulator is a dangerous game. It's like playing with fire because manipulators are liars and it's impossible to tell whether they will actually hold their end of any agreement you make with them. If you must deal with a manipulator, then make sure that they can back up every word that they tell you. Remember that in a Street Negotiation, trust is independent of tactical decision making.

A Manipulator Is Characterized by:

- Skill in using charm to influence
- Intimidation tactics when they don't get their way
- Use of guilt as a weapon
- Unethical demands
- Use of emotional appeals rather than logical arguments

Identifying a Manipulator

Manipulators are often people that we trust and that we think of as close-ones. Occasionally, it's a good idea to use the following 4-star test to see if someone you know might be a manipulator. If the person you suspect is uses one or all of these emotional appeals to bait you into compliance, then chances are that they have a manipulating personality.

Appealing to your love. The person will appeal to your relationship with them in order to influence you. "Just trust me okay? I love you and I'd never break our relationship, so just trust me on this."

Appealing to your guilt. The person will attempt to influence you by making you feel guilty about refusing their request. "If you love me you will do this."

Intimidation. The person will actually become angered at your refusal to comply in an effort to intimidate you into compliance. "I hate how you always question me like that. Just do it, okay?"

False flattery. The person will shower you with compliments in an effort to get you to comply. "You're the greatest person. What would I ever do without you?"

Can I Negotiate With a Manipulator

Bear in mind that the definition of a negotiation is a discussion of options between two people that's designed to leave one or both of them with something better than what they could obtain on their own. That being said, I'm not going to say that a negotiation with a manipulator should never be done, but weigh in the risks and alternatives associated with that negotiation. Think with your rational mind when dealing with the manipulator and base your premise on whether or not they can deliver you something that's better or less risky than what you can obtain without negotiating with them. Make sure that you don't base your decisions on emotional appeals, but rather on solid and measurable results and solutions that you can hold them accountable for. Lock them into a specific agreement that has identifiable boundaries and deadlines that can be enforced. Make sure that both that you establish penalties and consequences for non-compliance of that agreement.

The Complainer

Complainers have a gripe about everything in their life. This usually comes from the underlying fact that they are unsatisfied or disgruntled about their own personal life and goals. The complainer has a need for their concerns to be both heard and acknowledged.

A Complainer Is Characterized by:

- Dissatisfaction in their personal life
- Anger
- A desire to have their concerns acknowledged
- Makes demands
- Wants explanations
- Makes threats or bluffs
- Frustration

Techniques for The Complainer

The key to effectively dealing with a complainer is by using your *active listening skills*. The complainer wants to be heard and acknowledged—not ignored or argued with. You have to use your skills of empathy and try to understand what their interests and needs are.

Listen to their concerns. It's not enough sometimes just to fix the problem. The person has a psychological need for someone to acknowledge their concerns. Let them get all of those pent up frustrations out of their system before you address the problem. Listen and acknowledge what they have to say. Encourage them to keep on talking until all those frustrations have been let out. Ask questions to probe deeper into what their needs and interests might be.

Empathize with them. Imagine yourself walking around in their shoes and see the situation from their perspective. Empathy is an important tool that you can use to facilitate cooperation. Let them know that you understand their situation and make them feel important. Use empathetic statements such as, "Gee. That sounds awful. I know I'd feel horrible if that happened to me."

Ask them what their needs are. In most cases, you'll already know what the person wants, but ask them what's really important to them and use it to distract them from their complaints and dig underneath their positions for the real "meat" of the issue.

Paraphrase their concerns back to them. Repeat their concerns back to them in your own words. This lets them know that you have been listening and it allows you to confirm that you've heard and understood everything correctly. Paraphrasing is also a powerful rapport-building tool.

The Gossiper

The gossiper loves to be the center of attention in their personal social groups, despite the fact that their own personal life is pretty much boring and mundane. To achieve being the center of attention, the gossiper collects private information about others, usually given to them under an *assumed* agreement of confidentiality, and then shares this privileged information with everyone else just for the sake of making interesting conversation. The gossiper does not care about the reputation of others, only about enhancing their own social attractiveness by having interesting stories to share. Often times the damage to your reputation that is inflicted by their gossip is permanent and this is why dealing with a gossiper can be dangerous. The gossiper pretends to be a trusted friend and preys off your emotional need to be heard and acknowledged, but the truth is that the gossiper is not a trusted friend at all, but rather a self-centered person whose only interest is to be the "talk of the town."

A Gossiper Is Characterized by:

- Curious
- Self-centered
- Persistent questioning
- Talkative about other people's lives
- Boring lives (hence why they must talk about others)
- Reputation wreckers
- Pretends to be a trusted friend
- Offers a piece of fake info on themselves to get your info

Techniques for The Gossiper

The best way to deal with the gossiper is to keep your private information locked up and away from their reach. Before you discuss anything that is potentially hazardous to your reputation, take a close look at whom it is you are talking to. Is it a trusted friend who has proven their reliability in keeping your private information confidential? Are they genuinely concerned about you and your well-being, or are they only interested in prying out the private information that has caught their interest? Here are some strategies to combat the gossiper:

Identify the gossiper by their actions. Most gossipers are well-known for being gossipers, but there are a few who are not so well-recognized because they are able to cover their tracks fairly well. One of the surest signs that someone is a gossiper is when they start discussing rumors or private information about another friend or coworker in your social or professional network. You can be sure that if they are doing it to someone else, then they are also doing the same to you.

Gossipers can be disguised. They can be disguised as family members, friends, or loved ones. Just because they are close, does not mean that they are not a dangerous gossiper. In fact, the most dangerous gossipers are ones that are close to you because they are able to more easily access private information about you.

Gossipers invade boundaries. A true friend knows and respects your boundaries when it comes to private and sensitive information about you. A true friend will know not to persist in their questioning if they know that they are invading your boundaries, unless of course they are genuinely worried about your well-being, in which case such invasion is justifiable. If someone you suspect might be a gossiper persists in asking you questions about sensitive information or confidential personal news, then ask them why they want to know so much. If they give you a generic answer such as: "I just want to know," "Just because," or "I don't know," then I can bet money that they are a gossiper attempting to leach information out of you. If they get angry at you for asking this question, then this is a sure sign that they are a gossiper also.

Don't share your life with just anyone. We all have the emotional need to vent out concerns that weigh heavy on our minds. Be careful who you choose to vent those concerns out to because chances are that the first person in line for to satisfy that need will be the gossiper. Use your most trusted friend for venting or find someone who has no social connection with your life, or ideally someone who is bound by law or faith not to disclose information such a psychologist or a priest.

If you don't like their question then reframe it. If you are posed with a question that you feel uncomfortable answering and you don't want to get them angry, then reframe that question into one that you can answer by telling them:

"I think what you are trying to say is…"

This changes the question without seemingly like you are dodging it.

> Example
>
> **Gossiper:** So why did you break up?
> **You:** I think what you are really saying is that the relationship was never meant to be, right?
>
> **Gossiper:** Did you sleep with him last night?
> **You:** I think what you trying to say is that he is a good guy for me and you hope I hold on to him, right?

Gossipers will use the law of reciprocity. Often when gossipers meet your resistance to their probing questions, they will use the tactic of offering a "seemingly" private piece of information about themselves to enact the psychological law of reciprocity and make you feel obligated to share your own secrets. Don't be tricked into giving up information just because they did.

Gossipers use persistence as another tactic. They can be very persistent because of their curious nature, often making emotional appeals to bait you into giving something up. Don't give in to this tactic. Persistence in trying to obtain private information should be a red flag that the person is a gossiper. Tell them that it's not something that you want to share right now and make that the end of the conversation. Most likely they will whine and get mad at you, but stand your ground because it's better that they get angry rather than let them destroy your good name.

Humanize yourself to them. Gossipers often readily and carelessly spread your confidential life around because they see your life more as a newspaper or magazine that can be shared among people. One technique to combat this is by confronting the gossiper and telling them that it caused you much pain that they shared your confidential information and they violated that trust between you. Show them that you are hurt because of it and humanize yourself in front of them. This will make it much more difficult for them to continue their gossiping behavior.

The Back-Stabber

The back-stabber is a dangerous person because you don't suspect that they're your enemy until they ruin your life. They usually fawn over you by giving you an excessive amount of praise, but deep inside of them, toxic emotions of jealousy or envy have taken control of their actions. The back-stabber is a coward by nature. They do not confront you directly, but rather wait till you're not around and then they go to work behind your back, sabotaging, manipulating, and destroying your life. The worse part about the backstabber is that you won't realize who was responsible for it until your life and reputation are wrecked for good. Here are the warning signs that someone might be a back-stabber:

Do they have low self-esteem? Back-stabbers have a low level of self-esteem, so they try vainly to compensate for it by pulling other people down to their level.

They shower you with excessive praise. Normal praise is expected when you do something good that deserves it. The back-stabber will shower you with an excessive amount of praise when you really haven't done anything impressive. This should be a red flag for you.

Do they talk trash about their friends? If they trash-talk about their other friends behind their back to you, then there is a good possibility that the same person is doing the same trash-talking about you behind your back.

Are they overly interested in your life? Back-stabbers tend to immerse themselves in the very thing that they envy and that causes them pain, which could be you. Their attitude tends to be that if they can't have it, then they are going to make sure that no one can. In order for them to carry that out, they immerse themselves in the lives of the people who they envy or are jealous about. Some might even get a thrill out of being so close and yet being the coldest one of all. This sociopathic behavior has been documented to a higher degree in serial killers who revisit a crime scene, or even ask police investigators questions about what happened, because they get a second thrill from being so close to being caught.

Are they reliable in getting something done on time and correctly? If they always seem to be unreliable or seem to always foul up simple tasks or favors that you ask of them, yet they seem to get things done when other people ask them for similar requests, then you might be suspicious that they are deliberately sabotaging you perhaps out of envy.

Back-stabbers are Characterized by:

- Jealous
- Envious (a more serious form of jealousy)
- Inner rage
- Manipulative
- Deceitful
- Passive-aggressive
- Fawning
- Sneaky
- Untrustworthy

Techniques for The Back-Stabber

The reason why back-stabbers are so dangerous is because they disguise themselves as friends and often you never realize that they are an enemy until it's too late. Identify them as a backstabber, using the red flags listed above. Then use the following strategies to help resolved their behavior before they destroy your life:

Don't fight fire-with-fire. The back-stabber is an expert social ninja, skilled at the ways of knifing people in the back without being detected. Don't try to play the same game with them because they are more skilled at it than you are and they will use your failed attempts against you to further increase the damage to your life and reputation. Fighting back will only come back to bite you in the future.

Avoid direct confrontation—it'll bite you. Granted, back-stabbers hate confrontation and will probably stop their sneaky attacks on you if you go right up to them and confront them about it, but backstabbers are excellent liars and they might deny everything you accuse them of, especially if a supervisor or third party is present. To make matters worst, the back-stabber will appear calm and rational in front of witnesses and you will be the one who looks like the psychologically-unstable aggressor, making the backstabber appear more credible while you lose your own credibility with others. This is a risky approach to dealing with a back-stabber.

Use a parable to let them know they are responsible. A parable is a fictional story that is used to teach a moral lesson. Instead of directly accusing the backstabber of a wrongdoing, chat with him informally and relate a fictitious story or scenario that has all the back-stabbing components of what he has done to you, but does not directly relate to him at all. This has the same effect of directly telling them that you know what they are doing, but it does so in a subtle manner with no point for counterattack. The back-stabber will become very uncomfortable with this parable because of its ambiguously similar nature and it will cause him to stop knifing you in the back.

Example

You learn that your coworker Tom has shot-down your nomination for a promotion behind your back by relating some confidential personal information about your upcoming divorce to the division manager. Instead of going up to Tom and shouting, "How dare you spread rumors about my private life to screw up my chances of promotion," confront Tom informally and give him a parable. "Tom, my son's been really pissed off lately and I wonder if you know what I can say to him to make him feel better. You see, he has been working hard to get promoted to get the first string quarterback position of his high school football team, but one of his rival teammates went behind his back to the coach and told his coach that my son drinks too much beer, so the coach decided not to pick him as quarterback. He's been pissed off ever since and I am not sure what to say to him because I'd be pissed too if someone I trusted back-stabbed me. Do you have any advice on what I can tell him?

The Bureaucrat

The bureaucrat is the grunt of an organization, originally meant for government institutions, but has been broadened to encompass any large organization or company. Bureaucrats include customer service representatives, insurance claims filers, civil servants, social workers, airport employees etc. The bureaucrat typically views his clients as numbers rather than faces and is usually overworked and underpaid and underappreciated. Because of the large volume of contacts that the bureaucrat handles on any given day, they often forget who they are dealing with and you become frustrated at the fact that you know them, but they don't remember you. Bureaucrats love to use the "template method" of dealing with people, often filtering everyone's questions through the same greeting, the same introduction, the same sales pitch, etc. Often people get upset at bureaucrats because they get the feeling that they are speaking to a brick wall.

Bureaucrats are characterized by:

- Cares little about your happiness in life
- Sees people as numbers rather than faces
- Pushed for time
- Handles each person the same i.e. scripted procedure
- Hides behind policies and rules
- Cannot look outside the box
- May have trouble remembering who you are due to a large volume of contacts
- May not want to reveal anything about their interests

Techniques for The Bureaucrat

Be polite and respectful of their position. Too often, the first thing out of a customer's mouth is some type of accusatory complaint such as, "You people screwed up again." While your anger might be justified, remember that the bureaucrat might not know who you are and will be less inclined to help you if you are verbally abusive towards them. They handle a lot of abuse, so be nice.

Make sure that they have the authority to negotiate. Make sure you don't waste your time dealing with someone who doesn't have the authority to negotiate with you. For example, if I was at a restaurant and wanted to order a dessert from the menu, then I would ask for a waiter or a waitress to help me rather than going to the busboy or dishwasher. Choose to deal with the person who has all the authority to negotiate with you, rather than pass it up the chain of command as a courtesy for you.

Don't immediately go vent on the supervisor. One of the most common customer tactics is asking to speak to the manager. In some cases it works, but in doing so, you bring a lot of conflict to the party. Make sure you don't automatically demand to speak to their superior because the subordinate will perceive that as a direct personal threat against them and react defensively against you. Remember that it is human need-driven behavior to react aggressively if you threaten their essential needs and by asking for a supervisor without giving them a chance to help, you are directly threatening their job—their ability to put food on the table, so be mindful that you don't cause undo by taking it to the next level. Also, their boss does not usually have the sufficient background information necessary to make a decision on your particular situation and many supervisors do not like overruling the decisions of their subordinates. They are more interested in the level of service that the subordinate provided you with because their expertise is in management, not front-line service. So don't automatically default to the higher authority unless absolutely necessary, work with the person to achieve your goals first.

Make sure that they fully understand your situation. Explain your situation in detail and give them as much background information as possible. Make sure that they understand the problem you are facing before moving on to options and solutions. The bureaucrat needs to have a firm understanding of your problem in order for them to feel comfortable helping you with anything, so ask them rhetorical questions like, "Do you understand?" "Do you see where I'm coming from?" "Do you have any questions?" Ask them for feedback and acknowledgement, especially when dealing with them over the phone, to make sure that they are following you.

Acknowledge their expertise and ask for help. Treat the bureaucrat with the dignity of being an expert in their field and ask them for their expert advice on your situation. Bureaucrats constantly get verbally attacked everyday about being ignorant or not knowing enough, so make yourself stand out and treat them like they were the foremost expert in their field. This type of ego-stroking has the effect of boosting their level of self-esteem and it will drive them to want to help you even more.

Discuss the spirit versus the letter of the law. Often to prove their point, bureaucrats will open up a 900 page company bible or law book and quote to you section, chapter, paragraph, and line of the company policy on why they can't help you. As with any law or policy, there is some leeway for interpretation. There is the letter of the law—the specific words in that policy or law that dictate enforcement, and there is the spirit of the law—the specific intent of the authors who wrote that law or policy. You might want to point out that the policy is good and purposeful, but it does not apply in your case because of your situation does not conform to the original spirit of that law or policy.

Determine a fair standard. Discuss with them what a fair standard for your particular situation is. If you are calling them because of a product defect, then what is the fair standard of getting that replaced or refunded? Agree on what is an objective criterion through which to filter your options. This often works much better than aiming high and hoping to get settle for something in the middle.

Have your plan B ready. There is no formula for a 100% successful negotiation, but there is a formula for moving forward regardless of the outcome—and that is your plan B, also known as the best alternative to a negotiated agreement. Your plan B is the best possible option that you have available without having to deal with the bureaucrat at all. It gives you confidence and increases your negotiating power. Have your plan B fully developed and ready to go before dealing with a bureaucrat and you will not only have more confidence negotiating with them, but you will also be able to move forward regardless of the negotiating outcome.

3
Reading & Speaking the Language of Non-verbal Communication

Sometimes a simple smile can warm the coldest of hearts.

~Tristan J. Loo

Nonverbal communication is a key factor in any negotiation and an essential part of effective communication. In this section, we explore the dynamics of a field known as neurolinguistic programming (NLP) to understand what people are saying when they aren't saying anything. Linguistic researchers argue that over 80% of human communication is accomplished without the use of the articulated word. Body language, usage of space and distance, gestures, facial expressions, and tone of voice all play a part in how we read other people. As a street negotiator, it's imperative that you start building your skills in reading other people without listening to their words. We are trained formally and informally from a very early age to speak with words. By the time we are adults, we are so good at using verbal communication that we can mask our true intentions with false words. Deception, false promises, and true emotions can all be masked by the spoken word. However, we are given very little training on the usage of nonverbal communication. It's something that we just pick up informally through social interaction and cultural exchange. As a result, we have very little skills at masking those nonverbal cues as effectively as we can with our spoken words. A trained street negotiator concentrates on what the person is saying nonverbally just as much as what they are saying with words. I personally make it a habit to listen to a person's body language more than their spoken words because I have found that their body language conveys their true intentions. While this section of this book is not a comprehensive guide to neurolinguistic programming, it should give you some fundamental direction and insight into the art of communicating without words.

What's Proxemics?

The study of the communicative aspects of personal space and territory is called *proxemics*. Everyone is surrounded by an invisible zone of psychological comfort that follows us everywhere we travel. This protective bubble acts as a buffer zone against unwanted touching and attacks. Our comfort zone varies depending on who we are talking to and the situation that we are in. The amount of space that we use while interacting with others can play a significant factor in the type of interaction we have with that person.

Why Is Proxemics Important For A Negotiation?

Proxemics gives a lot of nonverbal information to the other person regarding the level of trust and intimacy that the person has for them. As cooperation is a key factor in Street Negotiation, you must be able to read their level of comfort with you by the amount of distance that they are comfortable dealing with you at. Your goal in a negotiation is to gain their cooperation and by knowing how personal space is internally regulated, you can foster better communication and cooperative behavior from your counterpart. Knowing the dynamics of personal space will also prevent you from unknowingly violating your counterpart's personal space and causing unnecessary tension.

What Is Our Comfort Zone?

In 1959, anthropologist Edward Hall discovered that humans are distinctly aware of our perception of space and territory and he conducted numerous studies and experiments in which he concluded that United States Americans had four distinct comfort distances, each with their own specific ranges of comfort, and that these distances were surprisingly universal to most Americans. He also noted that comfort zones varied drastically between cultures. The four distances of personal territory for U.S. Americans are:

> **0—18 inches.** *Intimate distance.* Reserved for deep personal relationships. Vision is impaired at this level and the main senses used are smell and touch. This distance is used for sexual contact or comforting someone.
>
> **18 inches—4 feet.** *Personal distance.* Reserved for personal conversation. This distance is used for having personal conversations with friends, family, or associates.
>
> **4 feet—12 feet.** *Social distance.* Reserved for formal interactions such as business meetings or interviews.
>
> **12 feet—line of sight.** *Public distance.* Reserved for such things as public speaking and lectures.
>
> *Note: These distances apply only to those interactions where the participants' orientation is face-to-face with each other and are aware of each other's presence.*

Avoid Violating Personal Space

The territorial space that people claim as distinctly belonging to them is their personal space (within 4 feet). When someone who has not yet gained our trust enters our personal space, we tend to feel uncomfortable or even threatened because the intruder has trespassed onto our own space. This is much the same way as if a stranger walked into the backyard of your home without your permission. Entering someone's personal distance without first establishing some level of trust can cause conflict and defensiveness to occur. When a violation of space occurs, it causes the other person to become uncomfortable and instinctively they will move themselves away from the person to regain the correct level of personal territory. You'll want to pay attention to this behavior because it is a sure indication that you have intruded upon their comfort zone. Often when an imposing male invades a female's personal space, she will either step back to regain that space or lean backwards to distance herself. Police officers are sometimes trained in the technique of deliberately invading the personal space of their suspect during an interview to make the suspect feel uncomfortable and intimidated into giving up information.

Proximity Separates the Strong from the Weak

Our social use for space can tell us a lot about the status, confidence, and power of the people around us. Just look at your own work place and examine who has the biggest office and who commands the most space while walking around.

The people who possess the *most* power and authority command a greater amount of personal space that they can call their own. They will often distance themselves from other people around them. In the workplace, the "important" top-dog might have their own corner office apart from the rest of the workers who might be scrunched together in cubicles.

Confident people, and people of higher status, are comfortable going straight to the center of the attention while lower status, *or non-confident people,* tend to hover near the exits or the back of the room. University studies have shown that the students who sat front and center of the classroom received the highest grades in the class, while those who sat in the back corner's of the room received the worst grades.

Are They Using Barriers?

Watch carefully if the other person sets up physical barriers between you and them during a conversation. Any inanimate object that is placed between you and the person you are talking with is an indication of defensiveness, or distance, because it subconsciously has the effect of creating a protective barrier between you and the person. A table, desk, pillow, drinking glass, pen, or even crossed arms and legs are examples of physical barriers. A person who creates barriers between themselves and the other person can be expressing deception, defensiveness, or ulterior motives. How do you get around barriers? Simple, just remove them. Of course you will have to be creative about doing it so that you don't offend the person. For example, when talking to someone who has their arms crossed as a barrier, drop a pen or hand them something—anything to break them of that barrier. Once the barriers are down, they will be more receptive to negotiating.

Using Proxemics for Emotional Emphasis

Proxemics can be used in combination with other behaviors to add emphasis to the message. For example, if a person is angry with you and they invade your intimate space, then the perceived threat of their anger is dramatically increased if compared with the same person being angry with you from across the room. If a couple are in love and they are maintaining eye contact with each other from across a room, then the impact of that eye contact is much less meaningful than if they were inches from each other. Distance can add quite a bit to the message being conveyed.

Where Should I Sit?

One of the main questions that people ask is how they should arrange seating during a negotiation. There is a bit of science to this that is grounded in human behavior and psychology. My experience as both a professional mediator and a police interrogator have strengthened my beliefs in the research that I have found.

The side-by-side position. Sitting side-by-side with your counterpart at the table is a task-focused position. It situates both of you facing in the same direction and pointing towards some type of work that needs to be done. The problem with this position is that you run the risk of invading the other person's personal space if a relationship is not established yet. One useful technique that salespeople use is not to sit side-by-side with their client, until another third party is at the table. When that third party comes to the table, the salesperson will then sit side-by-side with their client while the other third party takes the across-the-table position. This is psychologically acceptable to the client because now the sales person is familiar to them and the third party is the stranger.

The across the table position. Sitting directly across the table from someone creates either a competitive, defensive, or power-focused atmosphere because the table acts as a solid barrier between the both of you. This can cause either party to take a firm stance on a position and be unwilling to budge from it. This type of seating can make one side powerful and the other side weak by the differences on either side of the table. Picture for example an executive's office. If you are going into an interview with the executive, your chair might be very low and simple, while the executive's chair might be very high, luxurious, and ornate. The executive's desk will be covering the lower-half of their body, giving them that much more barrier protection, while you have none.

The corner position. The best seating position at a table for a casual exchange of information is at the corner of the table. In this seating arrangement, one person takes one side of the corner and the other person takes the other side of the corner of the table. The benefits of this position are that: (1) it brings you closer to your counterpart, thereby creating a stronger connection with them (2) The corner of the table still provides a partial barrier between the both of you which is comforting to the person if they are still unsure about you (3) It removes the formal distance of having the table separating the two of you.

Gender differences. A study done by Byrne and Fisher (1975) showed that American men generally chose to sit across from people who they considered their friends and American women chose to sit adjacent to the people that they considered to be their friends. Additionally, the study showed that men did not like strangers sitting across from them and women did not like having strangers sitting next to them.

The Tea Combat

A master of the tea ceremony in old Japan once accidentally slighted a soldier. He quickly apologized, but the rather impetuous soldier demanded that the matter be settled in a sword duel. The tea master, who had no experience with swords, asked the advice of a fellow Zen master who did possess such skill. As he was served by his friend, the Zen swordsman could not help but notice how the tea master performed his art with perfect concentration and tranquility. "Tomorrow," the Zen swordsman said, "when you duel the soldier, hold your weapon above your head, as if ready to strike, and face him with the same concentration and tranquility with which you perform the tea ceremony." The next day, at the appointed time and place for the duel, the tea master followed this advice. The soldier, readying himself to strike, stared for a long time into the fully attentive but calm face of the tea master. Finally, the soldier lowered his sword, apologized for his arrogance, and left without a blow being struck.

Your self-confidence in any negotiation is an important factor that needs to be there in order for success to follow. This comes with planning and knowing what you are going to do, say, and act during the conflict resolution process. People have an automatic sixth-sense for detecting a lack of self-confidence or fear. It may not be apparent to you, but it is very apparent to the people that you are interacting with. Police officers are taught the importance of command presence during their interactions with subjects out there on the street. It's a known thing for cops that the best experts in detecting a lack of self-confidence is not some Ph.D. sitting at a desk, but rather those hardened criminals out there on the street who spend their entire lives learning how to read people and sizing them up. People know when you are unsure of yourself—it's very easy to read. They know when they have the upper hand. Tell yourself that you control your own fate and it does not matter what the odds are or how many obstacles are blocking your path. Self-confidence can give you the power to clear that path to negotiating success for you.

Physical Appearance

Physical appearance is the first form of nonverbal communication we send to someone that describes who we are. The type of body we have and the way we clothe it can influence the way that others perceive us and the way they treat us as well. Types of clothing, such as uniforms, tell other people who we are and what we do. Gang members associate themselves with other gang members by the way they dress and commit acts of aggression, and oftentimes murder, on other people they perceive to be rival gang members just based on appearance alone.

The First Impression before the First Impression

Although what you say, how you act, and what you know is of ultimate value in any type of relationship, it is your initial appearance that is going to send the first message to people. Psychological research has shown that within the first 5 seconds of seeing a stranger, you will have already made some very important assumptions about their personality, status, wealth, popularity, and origin just based on how they appear. Your first impression is important because it enacts a powerful psychological rule known as the *primacy effect*. The psychological law of primacy states that your initial impression of a person, whether it is good or bad, will affect your subsequent ideas of that person. Think of making a good first impression as winning your first sale with your counterpart.

The physical attributes that people initially assess are:

Attractiveness. Provides assumptions on your popularity, social skills, likeability, and success. A sobering thought is that most people perceive attractive people to be more successful and trustworthy than their non-attractive equals.

Clothing. Provides assumptions on social class, personality, education, financial status, age, and credibility.

Cleanliness, grooming, hygiene. Provides assumptions on the person's health, self-maintenance, and social attractiveness.

Hairstyle and color. Provides assumptions on personality, health, age, and culture.

Height. Provides assumptions on the person's confidence or level of threat.

Weight. Provides assumptions on health, ambition, and personality type.

Race. Provides assumptions of behavior based on stereotyped ethnic beliefs that the person subscribes to.

How to Improve Your 5-Second First Impression

Look your best 100% of the time. Since you never know what people you might run into on any given day and what opportunities might present themselves because of it—you always want to look your best going out. Don't miss an opportunity just because you were too lazy to properly groom yourself.

Dress 10% better than your peers. If you want to stand out among the crowd without being showy, the general rule is to dress 10% better than your peers. That way you stand out from the pack in a subtle way. Dressing worst than your peers will make you appear less interesting, less professional, and less attractive. Extreme overdressing will distance you from your peers and make your counterpart feel inadequate and self-conscious about their own appearance.

Grooming and hygiene. Grooming and hygiene convey a lot of information about how stable our personal lives are. A person who does not shower, shave, or brush his teeth will be sending nonverbal messages that their life is not important. Keep yourself neat and trimmed to show others that you place a high value on yourself.

Score points with a smile. One of the easiest things you can change on your face to increase your attractiveness is to simply smile. This powerful nonverbal expression conveys a ton of favorable information instantly. Smiling tells other people that you are happy, confident, and enthusiastic. Psychological research into smiling has shown that people are highly influenced by a person's smile alone.

Keep your teeth white. It's interesting that people attempt to make their face more attractive through plastic surgery, yet they don't do anything to improve the quality of their teeth. Having pearly-white teeth is *the most effective* and least evasive cosmetic change you can do to your face that will improve your attractiveness several times over. This is because we associate the teeth with the positive emotional qualities of the smile as well as level of health, hygiene, and cleanliness.

What Message Does Your Body Type Covey to Others?

Body types speak a nonverbal language all their own. People will often associate particular attributes to your personality just by analyzing what kind of body you have. Take a look at these three classifications of body-types and see where you fit in.

Endomorphic. Characterized by round bodies and are usually heavy or overweight. People think of endomorphs as being soft-tempered, calm, and forgiving.

Mesomorphic. Characterized by an athletic build with broad shoulders and a tapered waist. Muscular in appearance. People think of mesomorphs as being confident, assertive, and self-reliant.

Ectomorphic. Characterized by a thin and bony build. Fragile in appearance. People think of ectomorphs as being tense, passive, and quiet.

What Does Your Hair Say About You?

Men

- Men with short hairstyles are perceived as more credible and more mature than men with longer hair. Men with long hair—being defined here as shoulder-length and below, are often seen as youthful, immature, and free-spirited. Statistically, men with shorter hair get more jobs and win more sales than men with long hair.

- Men who are bald (even if young) are seen as wise, mature, and responsible.

- In almost all cases, people are more agreeable with men without facial hair. Business studies have shown that clean-shaven men make more sales than men with facial hair.

- Any type of ear or nose hair sends an instant message of improper hygiene and grooming, which can destroy a first impression.

Women

- Women with long hairstyles are perceived as rebellious and sexy and often perceived by males as having a lower intelligence than women with shorter hairstyles who are viewed as being responsible, and mature.

- Women have the option; however, of putting their hair up in the office to gain the respect that they deserve, while letting it down when they want to be perceived as sexy.

What You Wear Is Important

In General

- Clothing sends immediate signals about your background, education, personality, financial status, and credibility.

- Women's shoes convey their personality and individualism, while men's shoes associate them into a category of membership (i.e. businessman, skater, hiker, cowboy).

- Jewelry conveys personality, social class, financial status, relationship status, and faith or beliefs.

At Work

- Dress codes and expectations differ from workplace to workplace, but follow the *10% rule* and dress ten percent better than the people you work with.

- Did you know that approximately 90% of employers heavily weighed their hiring decisions on the type of clothing an applicant wears to the interview? Even more astonishing is that many employers decide within the first 30 seconds whether or not the person is right for the job.

- *For men:* Business suits on men accentuate masculine attributes. A man's business coat is designed to widen the shoulders and slim the waist, giving him a powerful-looking V-shaped upper torso. The lapels flare outward, accentuating the look of pectoral strength. The collared shirt makes the neck appear thicker and conceals it from view because the neck is a vulnerable area of attack in the animal world. The necktie also conceals the neck and also makes the person appear taller by drawing a vertical line down his middle.

- Make sure that you do not have any pens, pocket protectors, or notepads sticking out of your business coat pockets as this can ruin your sharp image.

- *For men:* The best colors for men to wear for important negotiations are dark blue or any shade of gray.

- Tattoos and body piercings (other than conservative earrings on females) are almost universally frowned upon by employers at an interview, even if the tattoo is meaningful, cultural, or religious.

At Play

- *For Men:* Hats send a strong nonverbal message to others about personality, and affiliation. Surprisingly, the logo on the hat is not as important as wearing the hat itself. The mere act of wearing a hat makes the male feel a part of a larger group.

- *For women:* High-heels accentuate feminity by drawing attention to the delicate nature of her feet. High-heels also shift the woman's balance forward, resulting in her derriere to be 25% more prominent.

- *For women:* Men pay little attention to latest fashion or trendy clothing. What catches their attention are form-fitting clothing and strong vibrant colors.

- *For men:* Women are keener on fashion and are very color-oriented, so stay trendy and color-coordinated to make an impression.

Color Cues

The type of clothing being worn is not the only nonverbal message that is being conveyed. The choice of color conveys to people what type of mood we are in by wearing it. Take a look at this list of perceived moods associated with colors:

Red. Hot, affectionate, angry, defiant, hostile, lusty, exciting, sexy.

Blue. Cool, pleasant, sad, secure, tender, and calm.

Yellow. Joyful, cheerful, playful, unpleasant, hostile, dangerous.

Orange. Unpleasant, disturbed upset, distressed, defiant, hostile, exciting.

Purple. Sad, depressed, dignified

Green. Cool, leisurely, in control, confident.

Black. Unhappy, sad, fearful, intense, dejected, melancholic, grieving.

Brown. Sad, unhappy, dejected.

White. Joyful, cold, neutral, innocence, pure.

Pink. Cute, playful, sexy, calm, harmless.

What Does The Face Say?

The human face is our biggest canvas when it comes to painting our emotions. Facial expressions alone have the powerful ability to convey emotional status. Likewise, people are accustomed to looking at the face first for signs of the person's emotional state.

Smiling

The smile is the single most universally recognized gesture in the world and one of the most powerful. Smiling coveys happiness, confidence, interest, enthusiasm, and unconditional acceptance. Smiling sends the message to another person that you accept them no matter who they are. Here are the other benefits of using this powerful facial expression:

Smiling makes you happy. Studies have shown that the very act of smiling on its own has the power to change your own mood. The facial feedback hypothesis states that the act of smiling in and of itself can stimulate enough peripheral experience to drive your feeling of happiness up a small amount.

Smiling improves relationships. Whether it be at work or at home, it is simply difficult to be angry or harbor ill feelings toward someone who shows a warm and innocent smile.

Smile increases attractiveness. Smiling is the single biggest—and the cheapest, part of your face that you can change to dramatically increase your level of attractiveness. This is because a smile conveys enthusiasm, interest, and complete acceptance. People gravitate towards others who make them feel happy and comfortable.

Smiling is contagious. By smiling, you force the other person to return your smile and in doing so that person's emotional state will be raised. So in effect, you have just brightened their day.

Smiling enacts a leniency effect. People who smile tend to be seen as more innocent than those who frown.

Smiling is universally recognized. In every culture around the world, smiling means the same thing to everyone.

Facial Expressions

The number of different facial expressions are too numerous to list, but here are some basic, yet important facial gestures that you should know.

Lowered eyebrows. Disagreement, discontent, doubt, or uncertainty.

Raised eyebrows. Surprise, disbelief, uncertainty.

Tense lips. A sign of anger, sympathy, a change of heart, or a new idea.

Lip pout. Sadness or attempts to solicit sympathy. In courtship, the lip pout signifies harmlessness.

Lip wetting. Signifies sexual arousal, or dry lips.

Wince. Expresses pain or extreme dislike.

Frown. Anger, displeasure, or doubt

Eye Contact and Eye Movement

It's important to know that the eyes are constantly moving and translating the world around them into information that the brain can process. Because the eyes are so closely linked to the brain, they become very useful tool in interpreting how the person is thinking.

Interpreting Eye Movements and Eye Contact

Avoiding eye contact. A person who avoids making eye contact is usually thought to be experiencing dishonesty, shyness, or lack of confidence.

Staring. Staring at someone makes them uncomfortable because they become self-conscious, or feel threatened. Men often stare at women, who they are sexually attracted to, making the women feel uncomfortable.

Scanning. Scanning is a learned skill of sizing up everyone who is in the area around you for possible threats. Undercover and off-duty officers sometimes telegraph the fact that they are officers because they are trained to scan a room. Criminals who are about to commit a crime also scan for threats

Gazing. Gazing is associated with honesty and trustworthiness. Gazing also conveys interest and enthusiasm. Gazing is frequent in couples that are in love.

Breaking eye contact. A person who is experiencing discomfort will avert their eyes from the other person. Breaking eye contact before answering a question can be an indicator of deception.

Roaming gaze. Someone who is looking at everything but the person who is talking to them is probably bored or not interested in the conversation or the person.

Piercing eye contact. This is an intimidation tactic used to make a person feel uncomfortable. This is common among people who are angry. It is threatening and challenging.

Gazing down after eye contact. If the person has established eye-contact and then gazes down it is either an act of submission, such as in the case when a girl looks down before breaking eye-contact with a guy that she is interested in, or it is an act of deception because the person does not believe their own words that they have just spoken.

Winking. A gesture of mutual understanding, of a shared secret or a private understanding, while in a public setting. A wink lets you share something private with another person while being in a public setting, thus increasing your level of closeness.

Gain Rapport by Maintaining Eye Contact

The eyes have a powerful ability to influence behavior. It has been shown that gazing into another person's eyes will create an emotional bond or attachment to that person, even if they are a stranger. Use this to your advantage by looking the person in their eyes when speaking to them, in conjunction with the powerful tactic of smiling, and you will find that the person will be open to persuasion and influence.

You can tell how genuinely interested a person is in you by watching their eye movement. If they are maintaining good eye contact with you then their focus is on you and your conversation with them. If their eye movement tends to wander around the room or becomes easily distracted by other things in the room, then their level of interest in you in questionable.

Be wary of your own eye movement too because your counterpart will be watching your eyes as a nonverbal cue of where your attention is. Avoid looking at your watch, or watching people pass by you while the other person is talking, because they will interpret your eye movements as a sign of boredom.

The eyes automatically lock onto moving objects and people. This can be a distraction if you are having a conversation with someone in a restaurant. If you are going to sit down at a table and have an important conversation with someone, then let them sit on the side that is facing the wall or away from the flow of foot traffic so that they are not constantly distracted each time someone walks across their field of view.

Eye-Movement and Deception

Followers of the school of neurolinguistic programming (NLP) believe that deception can be tracked by eye-movement. There is actually a lot of supported science behind this and new eye-tracking polygraph machines are being used right now instead of the traditional polygraph machines that track breathing rate, heart rate, and galvanic skin resistance. In my opinion however, one cannot use these methods reliably in the field because NLP varies if the person is right or left handed and also how they interpret the question being posed to them. In short, there are too many variables to calculate whether they are telling the truth or not just by the direction of how their eye moves.

However, one can still detect deception without all the fancy NLP. These techniques come from the streets and are much easier and more reliable than any other human method of detecting deception. The premise is that a deceptive person will avoid looking you in the eyes because of the common belief that the eyes are windows into our souls and to look you in the eyes will be allowing you to see the truth. Therefore, instead of watching what direction their eyes move, just concentrate on their eye-contact in general. If they make a statement or answer while they break eye contact or if their eye movement is side-to-side, without ever locking in on your own eyes, then this is a good indication of deception. Don't confuse their break in eye-contact with that of submission however, as in the case with a flirting couple. The deceptive person will avoid making eye contact with you altogether.

Body Language

Gestures and body movement add animation to verbal speech. When we think about body language, what we envision are gestures and body movement. The scientific term for communicative body movements is kinesics. People use gestures to add emphasis to their communication, but kinesics also telegraph nonverbal messages about what actions a person might take.

Posture & Stance

The way we stand or sit and our body position conveys nonverbal messages about our mood, personality, and character. The three main types of postures are standing, sitting, and lying down. Here are the descriptions of the most common postures & stances:

Upright posture. Someone who is standing or sitting upright is sending a message of confidence, authority, and interest. Standing upright automatically makes a person taller and appears more youthful.

Slouching. A person slouches by caving their back forward and rolling their shoulders forward. This expresses disinterest or laziness. It is also indicative of their work in general.

Leaning back in a chair. Leaning back is associated with a negative attitude or lack of interest. Leaning back is also a show of dominance by the person.

Leaning forward. A person who is hunched forward at the edge of their seat is expressing interest in the conversation or the person, and is associated with a positive attitude.

Body position. Studies have shown that people tend to point their upper torsos in the direction of people who they are interested in, or have an allegiance to such as a boss. In courtship, a girl will unconsciously align her upper body with a guy who she has an interest in, even if she is not looking at him at the moment.

Looming. This is where one person stands above the other person. Most often, this occurs when one person is sitting and the other person is standing. Looming conveys dominance and power.

Open posture. Open postures—such as palms open and arms/legs uncrossed communicate warmth, trust, and friendliness. Closed postures do the opposite.

Bladed stance. A person who "blades" their body at an angle to the other person while standing should be watched carefully. A bladed stance is a prime position for an attack because it makes the person's torso a smaller target and they are well balanced. It can also mean that the person is untrusting of you and is on the defensive.

Gestures

Gestures involve movements of the arms, hands, torso, head, and legs. There are literally hundreds, of different gestures, which vary from culture to culture. Here are the most common gestures used in North America.

Head gestures

Head shake. Head-shaking from side to side means disagreement or disbelief.

Head nod. A person nodding their head in a vertical fashion means that they are in agreement. It also encourages other people to speak to you during a conversation.

Head tilted back. This is an over exaggerated version of keeping your head up high. In this case, the person is showing arrogance, power, and dominance over the other person.

Head-tilting. Head-tilting to either the right or left side shows friendliness and a willingness to establish trust. It is often used in courtship to display affection and submissiveness to the other person.

Head up. A person who holds their head up is showing assertiveness and confidence.

Head down. Someone with their head down is expressing shame, bad mood, sadness, or indecision. In other cultures, such as Japan, having your head down is a sign of respect.

Torso Gestures

Shoulder shrug. A counterpart who shrugs his shoulders is expressing uncertainty or submissiveness.

Arm Gestures

Crossed arms. Interpreted as a defensive signal. Might reveal nervousness, disliking, or defiance. Someone who is uncomfortable talking to another person will cross their arms as an unconscious self-comforting behavior because they have just created a natural shield (their crossed arms) in front of them. Psychologist Albert Mehrabian conducted a study where he discovered that women who were sitting and liked the person they were with had an open-arm posture, while women who were indifferent or disliked the person had a crossed-arm posture.

Hand Gestures

Hand to face. If their hand touches their face (lips, nose, ears, eyes), it could be a sign of anxiety or deception. If they cover their mouth while speaking, it can be an indication that they do not fully believe in what they are saying.

Hands on hips. Having your hands on your hips indicates that you are ready to take action, or take charge, or that something/someone is irritating you

Palms up. This gesture signifies that someone can be trusted and is harmless (showing that he is holding no weapons). It can also convey uncertainty.

Hand-steepling. This is where the person places the tips of his fingers together in the shape of a church steeple. He might bring his fingers up to his lips or drum the pads of his fingertips together. This gesture signifies thinking or contemplating new information.

Palms down. Having the palms facing down shows confidence, assertiveness, and dominance.

Clenched fists. Universally this is a sign of frustration or inner rage. Police officers are taught to be cautious when dealing with a subject who has his hands clenched or a subject who is opening and closing his fists because it is a psychological indication that person is priming themselves for an attack.

Pointing. Pointing can be used to direct someone's attention to something or someplace. Finger pointing conveys authority and emphasis. It can also be expressed as an aggressive or hostile act if done directly to someone at close quarters.

Fidgeting. Someone who is playing with a pencil or other object on their desk is expressing an unconscious behavior of nervousness. Fidgeting is easily identifiable to other people and can be annoying as well, but because the behavior is unconscious, you might not be aware that you are fidgeting. To prevent this, make sure you don't have anything in your hands when you are talking. This will prevent any playing around or fidgeting with items that can be distracting during a negotiation.

Leg / Foot Gestures

Legs uncrossed and feet flat on the floor. The person is open to suggestions and is willing to hear your ideas.

Leg crossed. It might seem natural, but the act of crossing legs is a highly unnatural act that is actually really uncomfortable when you think about it. There are many variations of the leg cross such as the ankle-ankle, ankle to knee, knee-knee. All of these represent similar meanings as the arm cross. Someone who has their legs crossed has essentially put a protective barrier in front of them for self-comfort. Often, people will try to appear calm by not crossing their arms, but crossing their legs instead.

Foot tapping. The person is expressing impatience, boredom, or nervousness.

Standing on toes. A person will stand on their toes when they have expressed something that they are excited or enthusiastic about to add emphasis to their point like an exclamation point.

Other Gestures

Throat-clearing. Represents uncertainty or deception.

Preening. Preening means essentially to groom ourselves to make ourselves look better. Preening behavior is an unconscious behavior exhibited in courting situations when we see someone we like and make initial eye-contact with them. Girls commonly run their hand through their hair and guys will adjust their tie or their collar.

How to Say More Than Words

The study of *vocalics or paralanguage* deals with the non-verbal qualities of speech. These include pitch, amplitude, rate, and voice quality. Linguists say that the way we say something often means more than what we are saying. Paralanguage instantly conveys things like gender, education, origin, mood, and our relationship with the person being spoken to. In our spoken language, only 7% of the total message is relayed through the spoken word, while 38% of the message is through paralanguage. Imagine answering a phone call from someone. If they are a close friend or family member, you can usually tell who it is without having them identify themselves. If it is a stranger on the other end, you can pick up certain things about who they are just by their paralanguage such as sex, age, educational level, origin, social class, even their attractiveness.

Interpreting Paralanguage

Emphasizing syllables. The way you say something can totally change the meaning of a sentence depending on what word you are emphasizing. Just think when the snotty kid tells you, "Whaaaat-ever!!" It's not only saying that she doesn't care, but it is also emphasizing a rebellious attitude as well.

Deepening voice. Police officers are taught to use a deep, clear voice because it carries more authority. A deep sounding voice is psychologically more believable than a higher frequency voice. Someone who lowers the frequency of their voice is expressing anger, defensiveness, or dominance because a deeper voice sounds bigger and it is linked to male masculinity and power.

Raised pitch. We raise the pitch of our voice to express harmlessness, submissiveness, and openness. In courtship, both men and women will increase the pitch of their voice above their normal frequency to make themselves appear less intimidating or hostile. The same behavior can be seen with friends, family, and especially when dealing with infant children.

Decrease in volume. A decrease in volume of the voice indicates submissiveness.

Increase in volume. An increase in the volume of the voice indicates anger, frustration, or a show of dominance or authority. Often when two people are arguing, each person will increase the volume of their voice to be louder than the other person; thereby, achieving a form of verbal dominance over them.

Speech errors. An increase in speech errors is an indication that the person is lying or not telling the complete truth.

Using Paralanguage for Your Advantage

Laughter. Laughter is a natural stress-reliever. Research has shown that laughter forces the body to release painkilling hormones such as *endorphins*, *enkephalins*, *dopamine*, *noradrenaline*, and *adrenaline* into our system. Laughter is often contagious and will brighten up other people's days just like smiling. It lets the other person know that they are your friend. Learning how to make other people laugh is a strong skill to gaining compliance from them.

Change their behavior with voice-leading. Voice-leading is a powerful technique that police use when trying to communicate with an irate subject. Often the person will be angry and they will be shouting at the officer and not making much sense. Instead of trying to have a shouting match with the subject, the officer will do the exact opposite and lower his voice down to a level that is difficult to hear. This accomplishes two things: (1) the angry person needs to calm down and become an active listener to be able to comprehend and process the words (2) the officer has stepped to the person's side instead of challenging him head-on (3) this behavior will force the person to mirror the officer's voice (4) it shows good professionalism on the officer's part.

Use a calm, clear tone of voice. To avoid sounding overtly nervous, slow down your voice rate and use a clear tone of voice when speaking. Think about what you are going to say before you say it.

Get rid of filler sounds. Filler sounds are the "aaahh," "uuuumm," "eeerrrr," sounds that we use to fill in periods of silence during our conversation. We generally use them when we are contemplating an answer. People have been conditioned to know that a filler sound means that you are searching for an answer, so they automatically take a "mental intermission" from the conversation and might not be paying attention to your answer. A more effective way of keeping them drawn into the conversation is by keeping the silence and saying nothing. Silence makes people uncomfortable, which has the effect of keeping their minds aware of what is going on, so by getting rid of filler sounds, you can maintain a better conversation.

Avoid a monotone voice. A monotonous voice is boring and puts people to sleep. Instead, talk with conviction and be enthusiastic about what you are saying.

A Touch Can Mean A Thousand Words

Haptics is the study of the communicative aspects of touch. In the United States, where touching is uncommon, communicative touch has a potent message in communication.

Touch is the most influential of all the nonverbal communication. A simple touch, even if accidental can affect us significantly. A single touch has the power of making the other person see us in a completely different way. The nonverbal communication of touch is much more powerful than the spoken word. Some would argue that it is the most powerful communication tool we have to convey emotions and attitudes. Think about it. There is more touching between people who like each other and more distance between people who don't like each other. We tend to touch more when our emotions go up. Through touch we can convey attitudes of friendship, love, sexual interest, affiliation, aggression, or disgust.

Categories of Touch

Psychologist Richard Hedin categorized touching into five main classifications.

Professional. This type of touching is necessary for a specific function such as a dentist giving his patient a cleaning. Note that a functional-type touch can be very intrusive on the body, such as a doctor's examination, but if the touch is deemed necessary for a purpose, then even the most intrusive touching still remains professional. Examples include:

- Body guiding (i.e. Coach correcting student's movements)
- Examination
- Arrest

Social. We touch in a social setting to convey greetings such as a handshake. It is the socially polite type of touching. Examples include:

- Handshakes
- Hugs
- Shoulder touching

Friendship. We convey a greater degree of warmth in friends by touching their shoulders, arms, or giving them a pat on the back. Examples include:

- The embrace
- Hand holding
- Body guiding
- The pat
- The body support
- The mock attack

Love. We convey non-sexual love through close body contact such as hugs, kisses, or touching of the head. Examples include:

- Hand to head
- Head to head
- Hand holding
- Kissing
- The waist embrace
- The half embrace

Sexual. Sexual touching is mostly restricted to the most erogenous zones of the body used to excite sexual desire. Examples include:

- Kissing
- Play-fighting (form of foreplay)
- Caressing erogenous zones

Tips on Communicative Touch

Touching increases fondness. The act of touching can increase the bond between two people. The caveat is that there must be some form of relationship between the two people before the touching occurs and the touch must be appropriate for the situation and the relationship, otherwise it can have the opposite effect and push them farther away.

Gender differences. Women are more comfortable communicating social touch to other women than with men. Men are more comfortable social touching women, but not other men.

Misinterpretation. Men are almost guaranteed to misinterpret a woman's friendly touch as an indication of sexual invite. In fact, a woman's touch to a man; outside a normal handshake can instantly create strong feelings of attraction to her.

Socially acceptable area for touching. The arm is the generally the only socially accepted area to be touched between opposite sex strangers in the United States. Even though it is common in other countries to be more openly about touching, the U.S. is a non-contact society where overtouching is considered taboo—or sexual harassment.

Back pats. A pat on the back can be comforting if a trusted relationship has already been established, but it can also be seen as patronizing or overbearing if the person is a stranger or of the opposite sex.

The first and last thing remembered. A touch, whether it is good or bad, is often the thing most remembered in a conversation or meeting because it involves tactile sensory input that the brain can easily recall.

How to Send the Right Messages With a Handshake

No wet hands. The most repulsive handshake around is one done with a wet or damp hands because it conjures up negative images of improper hygiene and fluid transfer. This will have the negative effect of starting you off with a bad first impression. Make sure you thoroughly dry your hands after washing them and discreetly wipe your hands on your pants prior to handshaking to remove the excess moisture from your hands.

No wimpy handshakes. A weak handshake is shows a lack of confidence and a lack of masculinity. The weakest handshakes are from men who deliberately play down their hand strength to women to seem less intimidating. Studies have shown that both sexes respect a firm handshake more than a weak one. A firm handshake is one where you are applying enough pressure that the person would not be able to remove their hand from yours easily. Don't confuse this with the ego-competing, hand-crushing practice of rival males.

Have web-to-web contact. A proper handshake is one where the web of your hand—that area between your thumb and index finger, meet up with the other person's web. This makes the grip more solid and it sends a subliminal message that you have the power to hold onto the relationship.

No two-handed shakes. Using the free-hand to cup the shaking hand or to touch their forearm while handshaking can be used to add further emphasis on the relationship; however, if that relationship has not been established yet, this form of "politician's handshake" will seem devious and insincere.

Cultural Differences

The range of socially-acceptable touching is different around the globe. There are two general types of classes: *contact* and *non-contact* cultures. People living in the United States fall under the non-contact group, because the socially accepted norm is that they tend to keep their distance from others who are not close to them. Often, these cultural differences can lead to conflict if one is not familiar with the customs of the visiting foreigner which could possibly happen in either a business or personal situation, so be familiar with cultures differences.

Some other countries which are *non-contact* groups are:

- All Asian countries
- India
- Australia
- Pakistan
- Northern Europe

The countries which fall under the contact group are:

- France
- Mexico
- Iraq
- Kuwait
- Saudi Arabia
- Cuba
- Turkey
- Italy
- Puerto Rico
- Brazil
- Venezuela
- South Europe
- Paraguay

4
Establishing Rapport, Building Trust

A person, who trusts no one, can't be trusted.

~Jerome Blattner

Rapport and trust are not the same. Trust is having complete and unswerving confidence in another person to maintain their integrity towards you and the relationship. Trust is built over a long period of time. On the other hand, establishing rapport is the act of trying to make yourself similar to your counterpart in an effort to create the initial building blocks of trusts. Building rapport is the first step in establishing the framework for confidence in the relationship. Confidence is the bridge that you must build towards the promised land of trust.

What Is Trust?

The word trust comes from the German word "trost" which means comfort. Trust is having the confidence in another person to be able to share personal feelings or information with them and not get taken advantage of. It is about giving them the key to your life, knowing that they can destroy you, but having the confidence that they will help you instead. The single-most important factor in gaining the voluntary compliance of someone is that they must trust you enough to have confidence that you will uphold your end of the agreement. No trust equals no agreement to a negotiation. Think of trust as your credit history when you are trying to finance a new car. No good credit—no good car.

The 15 Ingredients to Build a Trusted Relationship

Competence. This is how well you "appear" to be at you given job or task. Imagine going to a dentist's office for a tooth extraction and the dentist has to refer to a step-by-step guide on how to remove your tooth. Doesn't make you feel too comfortable does it? Likewise, you can also be seen as an incompetent friend or lover too. You can be seen as competent by projecting confidence and having knowledge of the subject.

Respect. In order for trust to be established, one needs to respect the boundaries of the other person. This agreement creates a solid foundation upon which further agreements can be built. Respect should be independent of whether or not you like the person. You can despise the person for what they are, like with a serial rapist or child molester, but you need to give them respect as a human being. Perhaps half or more of the people you deal with on a daily basis you wouldn't care to know on a personal level, but that does not mean that your personal feelings about that person should cloud the amount of politeness and respect that you show them. Respect builds rapport which creates trust.

Appearance. You have to look the part if you are going to establish immediate trust with a person or client. If you walk into the office of the financial advisor you want to hire to help plan your financial future and he is dressed in woman's lingerie; would you hire him? Your appearance creates the environment for trust to occur. If you are engaged in business then you must look professional. If you are looking for trust in a relationship, then you will have to dress to match their lifestyle.

Positivity. We all know the person who complains about how crappy his life is and how he hates the world and everything in it. This attitude is counterproductive to trust. People want to hear positive things like future goals and dreams because that inspires them and they can feed off that positive energy. Always be positive in life and you will find that it is easier to establish relationships and build trust.

Responsibility. There are no perfect people out there in the world and everyone makes mistakes. People know this and understand that it is part of the learning process of life. Trust is built on the basis that you take responsibility for your mistakes in life and learn from them and do your best to repair the damage caused by the mistake. By denying responsibility for the mistake or projecting the blame away from yourself, you are essentially telling people that you haven't learned from the mistake and that you won't help to repair the damage and that it will probably happen again in the future.

Listening. People have a desire to be heard—for their ideas to be shared by other people, so an easy way to build trust is to have an open ear. Let the person talk to you about their life and the stuff that is important to them. This will have a reciprocal factor of drawing you into their lives and building trust.

Empathy. This is your ability to see the world through their eyes by "walking around in their shoes." Empathy reduces the level of tension between both of you and facilitates trust building through mutual understanding. (Refer to next chapter for more on empathy.

Honesty. You want to be truthful in both your personal and your professional life. Honesty facilitates trust building by letting your counterpart know that what you are telling them is truthful and genuine. A trusted relationship is one where the person will risk making the other person upset by telling him something that they may not want to hear if they know it will help them out in the long run.

Patience. People don't enjoy being rushed through things. Patience equals comfort and comfort facilitates trust. Giving a client ample amount of time to think things through rather than pressuring them to sign the contract is an example of using patience to build trust.

Common interests. Having shared interests provides you with a forum upon which you have a basis to talk and exchange ideas. The more interests you share the better. Common interests are the best way to meet people because it's something that both of you know and it's something that both of you enjoy.

Enthusiasm. This is your level of motivation to making things work out. People want to be around other people who are motivated to forming healthy relations. If you meet someone for the first time and they give you the "shrug-off" or are looking around the room while you are talking to them, then that does not convey much enthusiasm to continue talking to them. However, if you meet a person and they take a keen interest in what you have to say by actively listening and maintaining good eye-contact, then you feel like they are enthusiastic about you and your life.

Loyalty. A trusted relationship is one where you can count on the other person being faithful to their word. A person who is loyal always holds their end of a promise. They have a high level of integrity to do the things that they say they will do.

Good communication. In order for trust to blossom in any given relationship, there has to be a good line of open communication between parties. Good communication involves making sure that your ideas are accurately "faxed" over to your counterpart and that miscommunication is avoided. This involves exchanging information between each other and over-communicating rather than under-communicating. It means telling the person how you feel and transmitting your interests, values, and goals so the other person can understand you better. Good communication involves the ability to openly discuss conflicts and issues that are inevitable on the road towards relationships. The other part of good communication is being able to read and speak good body language. You want to be sure you are sending nonverbal language that is consistent with your spoken words.

Security. According to Maslow's Hierarchy of Needs, people have a need to feel safe and secure in their environment. You want to help facilitate that need for security by projecting yourself as a safe and comforting individual. You can do this by presenting yourself as non-threatening, intellectual, responsible, and empathetic.

Self-sacrifice. Self-sacrifice is one of the most important components of a trusted relationship. Does the person sacrifice their own resources to help you out, with little or no gain for themselves? If situation becomes you against them, will they turn on you to save their own skin? You would be surprised at the number of close friends you have who would push you into the fire in order to save themselves.

Mirroring to Build Rapport

Research has proven that people find others who act similar to them as more likable than those who act differently. A good way of developing initial rapport with your counterpart is by using a technique called *mirroring*. Mirroring refers to matching your counterpart's voice, posture, breathing patterns, and gestures to be more like them. People who get along naturally are automatically in synch with each other. It makes the other person feel more comfortable with you and more willing to open up communication with you if you appear to act as they do. Mirroring allows trust to be established very quickly by opening up the channel of communication.

Mirror their posture. Take a look at the posture of your counterpart and adopt it as your own. If they are seated, then you will want to have a seat also. If their head is tilted, then tilt your own head in a similar fashion. Many police officers are accustomed to talking to people standing up, while the other person is sitting down, because it gives them a tactical advantage. This however, works against facilitating rapport with the person that they are interviewing. Experienced officers know that they can build a lot more rapport with a victim or child if they kneel down to their level and reduce their dominating stance over them.

Mirror their speech pattern. Match your vocal cues to that of your counterpart in terms of tone, pitch, volume, and speech to be in synch with your counterpart. If they are speaking slowly, then slow down your own speech. If they are talking rapidly, then speed yours up.

Mirror their choice of words or phrases. Many people have specific verbage that they like to use. Slowly incorporate these into your own talk to enhance rapport. Detectives use verbage mirroring when talking to children to establish rapport and open up communication.

Mirror their body language and gestures. If your counterpart has his legs crossed, then cross your own. If he has one hand in his pocket, then do the same. Be observant of the types of hand movements and gestures that he is using and incorporate those into your own communication with him.

Mirror their breathing pattern. This is a more advanced level of mirroring, but if you take time to notice their breathing pattern, and adjust your own to match theirs, then it will work to enhance rapport. If you watch any couple who are in love—they naturally will be breathing in sync with each other.

How Do You Know When You Have Established Rapport?

There is a proven technique for you to test whether or not you have established rapport with your counterpart. This technique is called *leading or behavior modification*. Leading relies on the natural tendency of people to mirror someone else that they are comfortable with after rapport is established during a conversation. Remember that mirroring is something that we unconsciously do naturally when we like the person we are with. You can take advantage of this unconscious behavior by adjusting your own nonverbal cues and seeing if they change their own to match yours. If you notice that they too change their nonverbal cues, then you can be fairly sure that rapport has been established. Here are some common ways to *lead*:

- Adjusting your rate of speech
- Adjusting your tone of voice
- Adjusting your posture
- Crossing or uncrossing your legs
- Picking up an object on the table

Other Factors in Rapport-Building

Mirroring is the first step in establishing rapport. The other half comes with your ability to listen and to empathize with them. Making them see that you are similar to them rather than different is the key to building rapport. Here are some strategies:

Treat them as equals. In order for a person to feel comfortable with you, it is necessary for them to see you as being similar to them. This is not always easy because their perspective, or even their lifestyle, might be completely different than your own. This is where you skills at empathetic role-playing come into play to meet them on their level. If they are poor, then you must be poor. If they are rich, then you must act rich. If you have a more powerful position at a company or socially, then you must dispense with that power. Use the power of empathy to figure out who they are and try to be like them. It will aid in facilitating rapport.

Active listening. Active listening is your ability to acknowledge and engage the other person in a conversation. The main power of active listening is that it allows anger and frustration to be vented. The second importance of active listening is that it creates rapport by establishing confidence in your behavior with them. Active listening is described completely later on in this book.

Make them feel comfortable. Fill their basic need for security by making them feel physically and emotionally safe. Avoid using aggressive or pushy sales tactics. Show your counterpart that you care about their comfort by offering them a drink and discussing their immediate concerns.

Make them feel welcome. Be enthusiastic about seeing them. Shake their hand. Tell them how great it is to see them. The important thing is to be genuine about it otherwise you run the risk of sounding fake. You always want to make the person feel invited.

Make them feel important. Give them your undivided attention when they are talking. Be enthusiastic about what they have to say no matter what the content is or how boring it might be to you. Orient your body position so that your upper body is directly pointing at them. This will let them know that you are paying close attention to only them.

Make them feel understood. Empathize with your counterpart. Let them know that you care and understand about their needs and values and that you consider their views important.

Important Trust-Building Strategies

Once rapport has been established, you must continue performing acts to win that person's trust and acceptance. Rapport itself is only the gateway for building trust. Continual practice of rapport techniques is what creates the solid foundation for trust to exist. Here are some strategies for building that bridge towards trust.

Be interested in what they have to say. Common sense dictates that people like to talk about the things that they are passionate about, and the things that they know. You can use their interests and passions as a platform for establishing a bond with them by talking about these things. What if you don't know anything about the subject? Even better, because the one thing that people love to do more than talk about the things that they are passionate about is to explain and teach those things to other people who are interested. So even if you don't have a clue about mountain climbing, show interest in the subject and ask intuitive questions that shows enthusiasm towards the things that are important to your counterpart.

Offer to help. The hotel industry recognized a long time ago how much repeat business and referrals they could obtain by offering to help their guests in any way they can. It shows confidence and trust in your counterpart by offering to lend help to them above the call of duty. That extra mile will tell them that you can be relied upon and that you consider them to be special.

Do it fast!! In this high-speed society of today—faster is always associated with better. Use this mindset to your advantage by making your counterpart's requests, tasks, and favors a priority and getting them done as soon as you can. Your speed in getting things done will be greatly rewarded with a greater amount of trust and an appreciation of your speed and reliability in handling tasks.

Invest time to build trust. Investing time into your counterpart and conversely having him invest time into you automatically increases your net worth to him because now if you walk away from the table—he stands to lose those hours that he has invested in you. By increasing the amount of time you invest into someone, you will be able to gain more cooperation from them.

Asking for help. Asking for help reaches that part of our emotion that wants to be noble and strong and compassionate. Asking for help acts as a trust builder because (1) it makes you seem vulnerable, so it lowers their guard and (2) by helping you out, it creates a karmic debt that you owe them, so in essence, you become something of worth to them rather than just a person. Asking for help is particularly useful when you are negotiating with someone who has all the answers and you are no match for their intellectual prowess. By asking for their help, you are no longer competing with them and instead, you are assuaging their ego and lowering their defenses at the same time.

Like them to get them to like you. People tend to like other people who like them. Even if they don't hold you in high favor, if they know that you like them or respect them or hold them in high regard, then they will subconsciously try to find a way to like you also. You can use this to your advantage by letting the person know that you like them right from the beginning.

Find common similarities and interests. Let's clear up a common misconception—opposites do not attract. Opposites make us curious. Similarities attract. By sharing similarities, you unconsciously set up a sense of comfort and familiarity with your counterpart that can become very powerful in building trust. Tips on finding Common Interests:

- Focus your conversation on the things that you share in common.
- Share similar experiences and stories.
- Avoid having to mention your likes and dislikes <u>first</u> in the conversation, just in case they are conflicting with the other person. Another strategy is to answer the question as vaguely as possible so that there is room for interpretation.

Ask questions to uncover common interests.

- "What do you like to eat?"
- "What things do you like to do in your spare time?"
- "What hobbies do you like?"
- "What do you do for fun?"
- "What kind of work do you do?"

Make them feel good. People tend to like other people who make them feel good. This is common sense, yet how many people do we know that try to buy their friendships in their pursuit to try to get the person to like them more? This is because what makes the person feel good is subject to the discretion of your counterpart. Ego boosting gifts (sincere praise, "at-a-boys," warm compliments, etc.) are much more powerful than any physical gift you can give.

- Don't mention negative things when talking to the person.
- Give specific praise.
- Remember things that are special in their lives (birthdays, family member names, etc.)
- Make your compliments genuine and sincere.
- Avoid compliments to sexual body parts. It only generates discomfort and makes you look like you're motivation is purely sexual in nature.

Drop the fancy titles. When you are out negotiating, it's always best to drop your fancy titles or letters at the end of your name because this might cause resistance from the other person. The moment you set foot on a used car lot, you know that you're defense mechanisms are going to work. Anything and probably everything that comes out of that salesman's mouth is going to be filtered through your raised defenses. Same goes if you are a police officer. Whether or not you are in uniform, once people know that you are a police officer, they will have their guard up around you because of that title. So when dealing with people, it's always best to be like them, or even better be below them, so that they will lower their guard and make it easier for you to make them see you as a person rather than a title.

The cases where you would want to showcase your credentials are of course when you are trying to influence people in a particular area with your expertise or when people are coming to you for help.

Is That So?

A beautiful girl in the village was pregnant. Her angry parents demanded to know who was the father. At first resistant to confess, the anxious and embarrassed girl finally pointed to Hakuin, the Zen master whom everyone previously revered for living such a pure life. When the outraged parents confronted Hakuin with their daughter's accusation, he simply replied "Is that so?"

When the child was born, the parents brought it to the Hakuin, who now was viewed as a pariah by the whole village. They demanded that he take care of the child since it was his responsibility. "Is that so?" Hakuin said calmly as he accepted the child.

For many months he took very good care of the child until the daughter could no longer withstand the lie she had told. She confessed that the real father was a young man in the village whom she had tried to protect. The parents immediately went to Hakuin to see if he would return the baby. With profuse apologies they explained what had happened. "Is that so?" Hakuin said as he handed them the child.

How do Gain Forgiveness From Another?

The best way to gain forgiveness from another person is to never lose that trust in the first place. Common sense rule aside, rebuilding lost trust is a difficult process with many obstacles to overcome—that is, if they *CAN* be overcome at all. Forgiveness requires absolute vulnerability on your part. Figuratively speaking, forgiveness can only be reached if you hand your partner an axe and place your head on the chopping block. Some might let you live…some might let the axe fall. Here are some tips on forgiveness and rebuilding lost trust:

Take full responsibility for your actions. Our normal inclination when faced with wrongdoing is to defend our actions, or make excuses or project the blame onto other people or events. This only works to make us appear even more at fault, because it puts us in a defensive mode and turns us into a target for even more scrutiny. Instead, take full responsibility for what you did without giving any type of excuse or deflecting the blame. Offer no resistance to them for attacking your past actions.

Give specific and sincere apologizes. A simple, "I'm sorry" will not suffice in facilitating forgiveness because it is too general and it does not sound sincere. Instead, make the apology specific to the wrongdoing that you have caused your counterpart. Tell them exactly what you did wrong and apologize for those specific actions. This will make the apology more sincere and facilitate forgiveness.

Acknowledge their power to punish. By doing an injustice to another person, you take away their power of control from them. You need to restore this power by putting yourself and your fate at their mercy. This will restore the power that they lost when you wronged them. By acknowledging their power to punish, you effectively "hand over" the axe and offer yourself up without resistance.

Actively listen. You will need to talk about what happened with your counterpart and diffuse any pent up emotions that are bottled up. You have to acknowledge what you did and apologize for it sincerely.

Concentrate on the future. Stop focusing on the past and concentrate on the road that lies ahead. The past cannot be changed or undone, so there is really little purpose to spend your mental energy keeping your mind set in the past. Acknowledge it and move on.

Show that you've learned your lesson. Concentrate on showing that your behavior and attitude has changed and you have learned your lesson. More importantly you must prove to your counterpart that this wrongdoing can never happen again.

Deception Comes Back to Bite You

One of the tactics you should stay far away from when you are negotiating is feeling tempted to lie to the other side to persuade them towards reaching an agreement. Lying may seem like an attractive means of compelling the person towards an agreement, but lying has a nasty tendency of coming back around and biting you in the ass. Sooner or later, the person is going to find out it's a lie and then any trust that you have established with the other side will be destroyed. Constant lying also builds up a negative reputation as someone who can't be trusted. You don't have to give away all your information to the other side and you should be wary about volunteering too much information, but steer clear from lying to the other person.

Just as bad as lying are promises that are either broken or forgotten. False promises are just the same as lying if not worst because a promise is a verbal seal of honor that binds you to that word. Promises build trust and are a useful tool when first trying to establish trust with the other side because you can exchange small promises and work up to larger ones. Broken promises are like a bad slot machine that promises riches, but never pays out. Sooner or later, the reputation as a promise-breaker will get around and no one will want to establish any trust with you. Some people use the word promise on a daily basis, with no real intent on keeping it. Be very careful around these people because they are most likely manipulators who make the offer sound more attractive than it really is.

The Promised Picnic

As a reward for his student's hard work, a teacher promised that he would take the student out on a picnic one day, but every day the student asked, the teacher replied that he was too busy today and promised the student he would take him on a later day, eventually the student gave up asking the teacher.

One day both teacher and student saw a procession go down the street carrying a corpse. The monk asked the student if he knew where the deceased man was going..

The young student told the monk, "He is going out on a picnic."

The Nature of Things

One day, a fox and a scorpion met each other at the edge of a small lake, both wanting to reach the other side. The fox could swim the lake, but the scorpion could not swim.

"Will you not help me get across the lake?" Asked the scorpion.

"But you are a scorpion. Surely if I let you sit on my back, then you will sting me," rationalized the fox.

"Ahhh, but if I sting you then we will both drown for sure."

The fox thought about this and decided that the scorpion made perfect logical sense.

The fox agreed to let the scorpion hop onto his back and then the fox began to swim across the lake. When the fox reached half-way across the lake, he felt a sharp pain in his back and knew that the scorpion had given him a deadly sting.

"You fool!! Why have you stung me?" The fox cried out. "Now we will both drown."

The scorpion replied, "Because I am a scorpion."

In order to reach an agreement, you need to establish rapport and trust with the other side so that they have confidence in your ability to keep the commitment. However, be cautious about the nature of the person that you are dealing with and don't be like the fox and assume that the person will hold true on their word just because it makes sense. Trust is an uncertain factor in a negotiation and placing too much trust in your counterpart will open you up to being taken advantage of in the future. Negotiations should run independent of trust because you can never tell if the facts, figures, and promises that are being quoted to you by your counterpart really is the truth. While the guiding principle of Street Negotiation is respect and cooperation, the other side might be using dirty tricks such as false facts and deception to throw you off guard. Or it might just be the case that the person's nature is similar to that of the scorpion and they cannot pass up an opportunity to take advantage of you because it is in their nature to do so. Don't give into these tricks by knowing the difference between earning trust and trusting the other side. When it comes to trust in a new relationship, whether it is personal or business related, it is always a dangerous thing to take the person for their word. The only thing you can trust in your negotiation is your level of commitment to the other side, so use that to earn their trust, while at the same time, be cautious about trusting them too soon. Make sure that they prove their trust before you start lowering your guard.

Effective Praising

All of us like to receive a pat on the back every once in a while for our efforts because it feels good and it lets us know that our efforts are being appreciated. In many places, however, the trend is to find fault and lay blame on our negative characteristics rather than our positive ones. This can lead to underlying resentment, bitterness, and even terrorist-like behavior against a company or person. Studies on work place violence have shown that the main reason why disgruntled workers engaged in hostile or terrorist-like behavior was because they felt that their job performance was being underscored by criticism rather than positive reinforcement. We often consider our basic needs to consist only of material things such as food, water, and shelter, but we also have a psychological need for praise that often goes unchecked by others. Praise is something that is a powerful motivating force that is highly desired by everyone and what's best is that it costs us nothing to give. The two main problems that most employers and supervisors make when giving praise is that (1) they combine both praise and criticism together, canceling out the positive effects of the praise, and (2) they often concentrate on giving very detailed and specific criticisms, while only giving general praise. General praise equals no praise at all because it simply does not register in a person's mind as being sincere. That is why many supervisors believe that they do in fact shower their subordinates with praise, but they fail to take into account that their delivery system for that praise is flawed.

Effective praising is credited to Ray Burke, Ph.D., a child psychologist, who found that giving specific praise reinforced good behavior in a way that general praising could not. In adults, the act of giving a general praise is often dismissed as being insincere because it alludes to the fact that the person was not really paying attention in the first place. He found that people associated general praise as just a formality of communication, to make the other person sound caring, but nothing more than that. He concluded that if we could make our praise much more specific towards the behavior that warranted the praise to begin with, then the effects of the praise would be felt by the individual and taken as genuine.

General versus Specific Praise

General praise. General praise is the form of praising that we are accustom to, both at work and in the home. General praise lacks any precise direction towards reinforcing a good behavior or action. General praise also lacks credibility because it takes no effort at all for a praiser to give a compliment without having paid any attention to the performance of the person. Most people associate general praise as a form of "friendly-talk" to make other people sound like they care, but rarely is it taken with any heartfelt appreciation.

Examples:

- "Good job."
- "Great."
- "Wonderful."
- "Cool."

Specific praise. Specific praise is a more effective and purposeful means of reinforcing positive behavior. Specific praise is the act of complementing not only the person, but also their specific behavior that deserves recognition. By making the praise specific, you not only make the person strive to duplicate that good behavior, but you also make the praise sound much more sincere because they know that you have been paying attention to their performance.

Examples:

- **General:** You're really smart.
- **Specific:** You really know your stuff when it comes to science. I'm really impressed.

- **General:** You're really a nice person.
- **Specific:** It makes me feel wonderful the way you take care of my problems. I really appreciate that.

- **General:** You're a great cook.
- **Specific:** I love the way you put so much attention to detail when making your dessert. It's that extra distance that you go that makes your cooking so wonderful.

How to Give Effective Praise

Make your praise sincere. Praise can be a wonderful motivating tool, but it has to be done with sincerity or it runs the risk of being dismissed as being fake or manipulative. You want to convey the praise with as much warmth and enthusiasm as possible. It is also best to give praise in person because most people perceive another person's time and effort as being something of high value.

Make your praise specific to the behavior. Avoid making any generalities about the praise you are giving. Before you praise someone, isolate the behavior that you are praising them for and praise that behavior along with the person. This will make the praise much more valuable to them and it will reinforce that specific behavior.

Praise sooner, not later. Praise can improve behavior in people, but its effectiveness greatly diminishes over time. Try to give specific praise as soon as you notice a worthy behavior. This creates an immediate psychological feedback association between the praise and the behavior which is still fresh in their mind.

Keep an eye out for praise-worthy behavior. Be proactive and watch for behavior that is worthy of praise. By doing this, you can reinforce good behavior when it happens and avoid correcting the mistakes afterwards in the form of a punishment or criticism which breeds resentment and conflict.

How To Give Criticism Without Bruising Egos

As responsible employers, parents, and friends, we have an obligation to correct the mistakes of other people in order to enhance their personal success. The task before us is how to correct a deficiency without damaging the delicate ego that can sometimes get in the way. Too often people criticize someone's behavior without providing a solution and this is detrimental because it then becomes a personal attack on the person that only aims to demerit them. Constructive criticism involves pointing out their weakness and offering a solution to correct it. In order to give constructive criticism, we must seek the solution to the problem before we point it out to the person. By doing this, we effectively separate the behavior from the ego and preserve the relationship in the process.

Here Are Some Strategies For Giving Constructive Criticism:

1. **Never criticize while you are angry with the person.** If your emotions are controlling your actions, then avoid any type of criticism. It becomes too easy to use that criticism as a chance to make a personal attack on the other person when emotions are high. Distance yourself and regain your own composure before you address a behavior that needs correcting.

2. **Offer a better solution.** Know the difference between disliking a certain behavior because it disagrees with your own personal preference versus disliking a behavior in favor of a more efficient way or correct way of doing something. Avoid making a criticism and then attempting to support it with emotional appeals because the issue then becomes a matter of personal preference and conflicting egos. Instead, use the power of logic to show the person that there really is a better way of doing the same thing that will enhance their own success and productivity.

3. **Always let the person save face.** This means respect the person, even if they did something completely inappropriate. The psychological consequences of embarrassing or disrespecting someone in front of their peers is very severe. It is so severe in fact, that such embarrassment has been a major factor in 80% of all violent incidents in the workplace and at schools. Criticism is a personal and private process that is not to be shared with anyone else. Also, it is just as important not to make it apparent to other people that you are giving, or going to give criticism. Asking someone to come into your office in front their peers can be just as damaging as criticizing them in public. Keep it very confidential and respect your counterpart's needs to save face in front of their peers.

4. **Focus on the problem, not the person.** When giving constructive criticism, make sure that you stay focused on addressing the problem and not the person. The problem is an objective issue that you can work cooperatively on to enhance both of your interests. Focusing in on the person, however, will always be construed as a personal attack against them—even if it is not meant to be. Personal attacks are always followed up with resentment and anger, which can actually be more detrimental in the long run because it can cause deep-seated resentment, which in turn, can lead to poor moral, clandestine or saboteur behavior, and passive-resistance. Remember that the person has feelings and those feelings can be easily broken by a wrong approach. Whenever you give criticism, follow the golden rule of attacking the problem, while being gentle on the person.

5. **Empathize with their position.** Empathy is the ability to step into the shoes of the other person and see the world from their perspective. Sometimes we forget what it is like to be the new person on the job because we have grown accustom to a certain procedure or routine that is second nature to us. Remember that people don't always see things as you do and part of being a good educator is being able to understand the other person's position and work with them at their level—not your own.

6. **Never label the person.** Attaching a negative label on the person being criticized is an inappropriate approach because it dehumanizes them, making it easier for you to be angry with them and it demoralizes them.

7. **Focus on the future, not the past.** Blaming someone for their past behavior does nothing but create conflict. The past is over with and your main concern is that it does not happen in the future. So instead of dwelling on past behavior, use it as a teaching tool so that they can improve in the future.

8. **Use softening words to pad your criticism.** Softening words are designed to "soften" harsh-sounding statements.. Softeners work because they leave a lot of room for interpretation of the statement that follows it. Some examples of softeners are, "I think," "I suppose," "it seems," "I believe," etc. So instead of making a harsh statement such as, "You're report is terrible." Replace it with a softened criticism such as, "It seems to me that this part of your report could use some revision." The psychological effect of rewording a statement can lead to a greater amount of persuasion and conflict avoidance.

9. **Give them an opportunity to correct their behavior.** This is an important step for any criticism because it works at two different levels. On the first level, giving them the opportunity to correct their behavior or actions lets them take responsibility for their behavior and reinforces the point that they must be held accountable for their actions. On the second level, giving them the opportunity to correct their behavior will give them an opportunity to redeem themselves and save face with you, which will make it easier for them to put their past behavior behind them and move one.

10. **Constructive criticism is a sign of compassion.** Criticism is often associated as a negative thing because it is often abused as a transport device for personal attacks. However, constructive criticism is a positive gift because the core message behind that criticism is that you care about the person enough to want them to succeed in the future. Constructive criticism is one of the main tests that separate regular people from true caring friends. Caring people will be honest with you and even risk generating conflict if they believe that their constructive criticism will help improve your life. Make sure that the person knows that your constructive criticism is done because you care about them and that you value your relationship with them. They will respect you more for being honest with them.

Part II
Turn Anger into Agreement in 6 Easy Steps

In Part II, you will learn the six-step P.E.R.P.O.S. system of negotiating a conflict into a successful agreement with anyone.

P lan Ahead

E motional Control

R educing Tension

P ersuade

O ptions

S olutions

Step I

Plan Ahead
E
R
P
O
S

Failing to Prepare is Preparing to Fail.

~Sun Tzu

Develop a Back-up Plan

Step one of the PERPOS system is creating your back-up plan, or what I refer to as your "plan B." Having a plan B in place before you negotiate a conflict will give you the confidence of being able to move forward even if you don't reach an agreement with your counterpart. It's a crucial step in the negotiating process and one that cannot be overlooked. Think of having a plan B in the same way an investor operates by diversifying his assets. He could put all of his money in an aggressive stock and risk losing all of it because the company is unstable, or he can put some of his assets into the aggressive stock and put some into a stable mutual fund with a proven growth record. Having a plan B is like diversifying your assets—instead of putting all of your assets into one basket, you spread them out so that if the main stock collapses, then you still have money left.

The Hostage Negotiator's Alternative

In a police tactical situation involving a hostage taker, a crisis negotiator will try to negotiate the safe release of the hostages and have the suspect surrender himself peacefully without any injury or loss of life. The negotiator's alternative should the negotiation fail is that the tactical team moves in and attempts to regain control of the situation by using force. This is the negotiator's best alternative plan if negotiations fail. The crisis negotiator's plan B is important because it gives him a great amount of control and confidence in the negotiation. Even though the suspect has hostages and believes that he is holding all the cards, the negotiator has some real bargaining power to bring the suspect back to the negotiating table. Both the police and the offender want to avoid a direct physical confrontation because it involves risk and the possibility of loss of life on either side, including the hostages. The negotiator has the option of terminating negotiations if things are not going well and falling back on the plan B (the SWAT team), but his main job is to try and reach a better solution than what can be achieved by using his plan B. Like the crisis negotiator, you too can use the same strategy of having a back up plan to increase your own negotiating power with a counterpart who seems to be holding all the cards.

Advantages of Having a Back-Up Plan

Fisher and Ury in their book, *Getting To Yes* use the term Best Alternative to a Negotiated Agreement (BATNA). Simply put, your BATNA, or plan B, is your next best alternative should negotiations fail. It is also known as your "walk-away alternative" because it gives you the power to be able to walk away from the negotiation at any time if you feel that the discussion will not present an option that is better than your back up plan. Here are the advantages of having a plan B:

- It protects you from being guided into an agreement that puts you in a worse position than when you first started.
- It gives you more leverage to negotiate with someone with more power than you.
- It gives you the confidence and the reassurance that you will be able to move forward independent of reaching an agreement.
- It gives you a basis for establishing a bottom line—your tripwire that lets you know when you should consider walking away from the table.
- It lets you know whether or not you should negotiate in the first place.

If you're negotiating for a raise from your boss, a possible plan B might be that you have another job offer from a different employer. If you're a parent negotiating with your rebellious son about doing his chores, then a possible plan B is to ground him. Regardless of the situation, you always need to have a backup plan prior to dealing with a conflict, otherwise you run the risk of putting all your assets into one plan that might end up collapsing on you and leaving you with no other recourse.

The Stone Cutter

There was once a stone cutter who was dissatisfied with himself and with his position in life. One day he passed a wealthy merchant's house. Through the open gateway, he saw many fine possessions and important visitors. "How powerful that merchant must be!" thought the stone cutter. He became very envious and wished that he could be like the merchant. To his great surprise, he suddenly became the merchant, enjoying more luxuries and power than he had ever imagined, but envied and detested by those less wealthy than himself. Soon a high official passed by, carried in a sedan chair, accompanied by attendants and escorted by soldiers beating gongs. Everyone, no matter how wealthy, had to bow low before the procession. "How powerful that official is!" he thought. "I wish that I could be a high official!"

Then he became the high official, carried everywhere in his embroidered sedan chair, feared and hated by the people all around. It was a hot summer day, so the official felt very uncomfortable in the sticky sedan chair. He looked up at the sun. It shone proudly in the sky, unaffected by his presence. "How powerful the sun is!" he thought. "I wish that I could be the sun!"

Then he became the sun, shining fiercely down on everyone, scorching the fields, cursed by the farmers and laborers. But a huge black cloud moved between him and the earth, so that his light could no longer shine on everything below. "How powerful that storm cloud is!" he thought. "I wish that I could be a cloud!"

Then he became the cloud, flooding the fields and villages, shouted at by everyone. But soon he found that he was being pushed away by some great force, and realized that it was the wind. "How powerful it is!" he thought. "I wish that I could be the wind!"

Then he became the wind, blowing tiles off the roofs of houses, uprooting trees, feared and hated by all below him. But after a while, he ran up against something that would not move, no matter how forcefully he blew against it - a huge, towering rock. "How powerful that rock is!" he thought. "I wish that I could be a rock!"

Then he became the rock, more powerful than anything else on earth. But as he stood there, he heard the sound of a hammer pounding a chisel into the hard surface, and felt himself being changed. "What could be more powerful than I, the rock?" he thought.

He looked down and saw far below him the figure of a stone cutter.

Empowering Your Alternative

Deciding on your plan B is only half the game. The other half is empowering your plan B by developing it into something that is real. Most people are good at thinking of creative alternatives to fill their needs, but they often fail to take the necessary steps to develop those ideas into something tangible. This is problematic because it gives them a false sense of how powerful or weak their plan B really is. For example, people always assume that if someone does not pay, then the best recourse is to take them to court. They fail to take into account the extremely long process it takes and the volume of paperwork and legal expenses necessary to take someone to court. They have failed to examine how powerful their backup plan really is because they did not take the necessary steps towards researching and empowering that plan B into something that could be used immediately. When a police crisis negotiator is on the phone with a hostage taker, the negotiator does not tell the commander to assemble the tactical unit later on when he feels that things might go bad. No, the tactical team is already there analyzing building schematics, points of entry, and developing a strategic plan that can be implemented the moment the order is given to move in. Likewise, if you're engaged in a salary negotiation with your boss, then your empowered plan B may involve having a job offer from another employer instead of the non-empowered plan of looking for a new job if you don't get a raise. Bringing that plan B into the real world and making it a true possibility is what infuses that alternative plan with power.

Identify, create, and empower your plan B using these three questions as your guide:

- What is the best deal that I can get on my own without negotiating?
- What steps do I need to take to make my plan B immediately executable?
- Can I walk away and immediately put my plan B into action?

Let Your Plan B Tell You Whether or Not you Should Negotiate

Is there a time when you should not negotiate? The answer is that your plan B will dictate whether or not you should negotiate. Remember that your plan B is the best solution that you can come up with on your own, independent of any help from your negotiating counterpart. Once you have your plan B fully developed, then you can ask yourself the important question, "Can they offer me anything better than what I can get on my own?" If the answer is 'yes' then negotiation is worthwhile. If the answer is 'no' then it suits your time and effort to forget about negotiating and implement your plan B into action. You always have the choice to negotiate or not, but let your plan B tell you whether it is worth it or not.

Keep Your Back-Up Plan Confidential

A professional poker player never reveals his hand. Whether he has a royal flush or nothing at all, the poker player keeps his game face on so that the other players can't tell what cards he is holding. The same is true for you and your plan B. Think of your plan B as your poker hand and you want to keep it hidden from the view of your counterpart. You never want to reveal what your plan B is because then your counterpart can judge whether or not their alternative plan is better than yours and they can take preventative measures against your plan B before you implement it. Some negotiators argue that it builds trust and cooperative problem-solving to lay your plan B out there on the table and they indeed have a good point, but that is putting a lot of trust into your counterpart and opens you up to being taken advantage of. Being open about interests and needs is fine, but keeping your plan B confidential is being street smart.

When a hostage negotiator is on a drop-phone with a terrorist, the negotiator does not give up his plan B by telling the terrorist that in exactly five minutes the SWAT team of seven officers are going to make an entry into the building through the West door, using a flash bang grenades and that there is a police sniper with a view of the Southwest window. Why? Because the terrorist can use the next 5 minutes to prepare for and set countermeasures against the SWAT team's assault. For the exact same reasons, you should never give up your plan B to your counterpart because they might set up countermeasures to render your plan B ineffective. Let them guess what it might be. Here are the advantages of keeping your plan B confidential:

- Avoids having your counterpart interpret your plan B as a threat.
- Prevents your counterpart from taking countermeasures against your backup plan.
- Prevents you from accidentally bargaining your plan B away on the negotiating table.

Be Able to Walk Away From the Negotiating Table

In any negotiation, the person who is least committed to the outcome has the most power because they can just pack up and walk out the door. Your Plan B gives you that power to be able to walk out that door, so it is crucial that you develop that Plan B before you sit down at the table. If you are tied down to the negotiation either financially or emotionally, then you will start making concessions that you otherwise would not give up just to close the deal. Having a "walk-away" alternative empowers you with a lot of negotiating muscle.

Establish Your Bottom Line

Your *bottom line* is the minimal amount of needs, beyond your plan B, that must be met in order for your agreement to happen. Think of your bottom line as the margin of profit that will make the negotiation worth your time and effort? Remember that your plan B is the best deal that you can get for yourself without having to deal with the other person. Your bottom line is merely the alarm that tells you when you should consider walking away from the deal because the value in no longer in your favor. Consider the following when creating your bottom line:

- What is your plan B?
- How much above your plan B do you want to set your bottom line?
- What are the soft costs of the negotiation (i.e. time, travel, stress, etc.)? And how can I build my bottom line to compensate me for these costs?

Anticipate Your Counterpart's Alternatives

Part of your planning will involve anticipating what your counterpart's alternatives are. By anticipating what their plan B is, you can get an idea about what their negotiating range might be and seek solutions that are more attractive than what their plan B offers them. Also, by anticipating your counterpart's plan B, you can prepare yourself if they choose to threaten you with their plan B (i.e. lawsuit, overcharging, etc.). To help anticipate your counterpart's plan B, ask yourself these questions:

- What is their current status, resource level, and dedication towards their goal?
- What is the best deal they can achieve for themselves without talking to you at all?
- Can you come up with a solution that suits your needs and at the same time offer something more attractive than what your counterpart can get on his own?

How to Uncover Your Interests—*and Theirs*

Identifying and developing your plan B is only the first half of step one. The other half is analyzing what your interests and goals are. The importance of having goals during a negotiation is to maintain your focus and objectivity throughout the process. Identifying goals are crucial for giving you a roadmap towards an agreement. Otherwise, you will lose your direction and open yourself up to being taken advantage of by your counterpart. Always plan ahead and map out exactly what you want out of the negotiation and you will always have something to shoot for while talking. Your personal goals will also help you focus on what is important when negotiations become difficult. To develop your goals, ask yourself these three questions:

- What do I hope to achieve by negotiating?
- Is it reasonable to expect that I can obtain something better by negotiating than if I did not negotiate at all?
- Is my goal reasonable and fair?

Positional Versus Interest-Based Negotiating

Positional negotiating. In positional negotiating, the parties begin by discussing their specific *wants* and then they attempt to compromise between competing proposals by making concessions. If any solution is reached, then it usually is a compromise between the two demands. The more the negotiator focuses on trying to change the other side's proposal, the more his counterpart aggressively defends his own ideas and attacks the other party's ideas to assert their own power. Positional negotiators often become frustrated with each other because the only way they feel they can reach the other person is by trying to break down their counterpart's defenses by attacking them, which usually ends up with little or no gain and a broken relationship to remember it by. Here are some examples of positional negotiating:

A car salesman and a customer meet at the dealership. The customer finds a car that he really likes and asks the salesman how much it costs. The salesman throws out a high number (high-balling) knowing he can work down from there. The customer knows that the salesman is throwing out a high number and combats it with a low buying price (low-balling) to bring him down. This battle of numbers goes on until they compromise on a price, or the customer leaves the dealership without the car.

A customer wants to buy a flowerpot at a swap meet from a vendor. The customer asks how much it costs. The vendor tells the person $10.00. The customer tells the vendor that the flowerpot is chipped and offers $2.50. The vendor scoffs at that amount saying that he'd be losing money. The vendor offers it for $7.50. The customer offers $5.00 and tells the vendor to "take it or leave it." The vendor says he just can't sell it for that amount and no sale is made.

Interest-based negotiating. In an interest-based negotiation, the parties start by discussing their underlying interests, needs, fears, and motivations first and then identify several options that might satisfy both of the negotiator's needs. Finally one option is agreed upon and made into a solution to the problem. Here are some examples of interest-based negotiating:

A husband is having an argument with his wife over the fact that he spends more time with his buddies than he does with her. She does not want him to go out. He promised his good friend that he would help him celebrate his new job promotion. Rather than argue about staying or leaving, the husband talks to his wife and listens to her concerns. After talking with her, he discovered that yesterday she had prepared a fancy dinner for him and he came home late and ruined her romantic dinner plans and that she was still bitter over this. He agrees to spend more time with her and keeps his promise with his friend by having his wife accompany him to the celebration.

A father and son are arguing over the rights to use the car. The father does not want to pay his son's car insurance. The son has just gotten his drivers license and wants to drive to school rather than take the bus. The father proposes that if the son can pay for his own car insurance, then he can have free access to the car. This solution satisfied the need of the father (money for car insurance) and satisfied the needs of the son (having a car to drive).

Why Positional Negotiating Creates Problems

The problem with positional negotiating is that each person digs into their set demands and the negotiation table becomes more like a battlefield of egos instead of a place of cooperation. The inherent problem with any type of positional bargaining is that it becomes less of a matter of solving the problem and more of a contest on who holds the most power. Positional bargaining is inefficient because it relies on making concessions. Neither side wants to concede anything because concessions are unconsciously thought of as losing the battle and human behavior, as well as common sense, dictates that no side wants to lose face with their peers. The person who makes the most concessions is seen as the loser and the person who makes the least amount of concessions is viewed as the winner. This creates an environment where negotiators are pitted against each other rather than working together to solve the problem.

When negotiating, you want to focus your discussion on your counterpart's interests rather than their positions. Don't just accept their proposal as their final answer because it represents only one option out of several undiscovered solutions that will satisfy their needs. Your goal is then to attempt to uncover their hidden motivations and reasons why they are making a demand in the first place. What problem are they trying to solve by stating their position?

Discover Your Interests underneath Your Positions

Most conflicts are started because the involved parties start by making a demand and then attempt to get the other side to give in using power and force. This is not only inefficient, but it also leads to even more conflict and anger towards the other person, because it takes a substantive problem and turns it personal. A more efficient way of negotiating a conflict is to first identify your interests behind your position and then discuss what options are available to meet those interests. Interests are your underlying needs that are hidden behind the positions that you make in a negotiation. If the other side offers you $10,000 for your car and you tell them that you want $15,000 for it—why specifically that amount? Why is $15,000 the magic number for you? Your interest might be that $15,000 is the amount you need to cover your debts, or that $15,000 is the fair market value of the car. Before you state your position to your counterpart, first ask yourself why you are stating that position in the first place and also ask yourself what problem is being solved by making this specific demand.

Behind every position, there is a problem that the position seeks to solve. When a conflict happens, it is because people tend to lock themselves into that position and fight dearly to protect it. What many people don't realize is that their position is only one way of solving the problem, when in fact there might be several creative ways to tackle that same problem. To find these options, you are going to need the cooperation of your counterpart. You want to begin your negotiations with a discussion of your interests rather than your positions. To uncover your interests ask yourself these questions:

- Why do I want that?
- Why am I making this demand?
- What problem is this position solving?

Identify Possible Options

Options are the creative ways that you can think of to satisfy your needs and interests. Your objective in any conflict is to come up with options that both satisfy your interests and also those of your counterpart. This is known as the best possible agreement. Creativity is important when considering options because there might be many unique ways of thinking outside the box and coming up with options that are innovative. Think of low-cost, high-gain tradeoffs that will satisfy your goals and that of your counterpart.

Consider Fair Standards

Creative options that you think of might satisfy your own goals, but what about the goals of the other person? Conflict is often generated when people have opposing views on fairness. Most of the time there is not an objective third party standing by to decide on fairness issues. Therefore, the next best thing to have is a neutral and objective standard to which to filter your options. A fair standard is a benchmark, or measuring stick, that you can use to gauge the fairness of your options. Fair standards can come in the form of fair market values, court rulings, laws, policies, competitor's practices, and even rational thought. By analyzing what makes your options fair, you can better negotiate with your counterpart.

Identify the Other Side's Interests

No two people ever see the same thing in exactly the same way. The classic example of one person seeing a glass of water as half empty, while another person seeing it as half full illustrates the importance of perspective in negotiations. Empathy, as you will learn later, is one of the most important factors in conflict resolution because it allows you to gain the perspective of your counterpart and look at the situation from their point of view. Metaphorically, empathy allows you to walk around in your counterpart's shoes. Use the power of empathy to rationalize what their interests might be. You might find that while your demands and positions are conflicting—many of your underlying interests will be the same. Ask yourself these questions to rationalize what their interests might be:

- What are the contributing factors that make them see the situation different from you?
- What is going on in their lives that affect their decision making?
- What do you know of their reputation, background, and personality that contributes to their perspective?

What Kind Of Negotiating Power Do You Have?

Most of the time when you enter a negotiation, it would seem that the other side is holding all the cards and you might ask yourself, "How can I possibly negotiate anything in such a miserable position?" This, however, is not always true. You possess much more power than just the positional power that you have going into the negotiation. Many people automatically assume that just because they are negotiating with a boss or with a company that they are automatically fighting an uphill battle likened to that of David and Goliath. Positional power is only one type of power. By planning and preparing, you can dramatically increase your negotiating leverage.

Positional Powers

Positional powers are the powers that each side is naturally endowed with in a negotiation. For instance, if it is a supervisor you are dealing with, then their positional power is their authority and status over you. If you are in a fight with a 300-pound guy, then his size over you is his positional power. These powers cannot be changed—you either have them or you don't, but that does not mean that you are automatically at a disadvantage. Having a good positional power will help make the negotiating process easier for you. Think of your positional power as training for a fight.

Being fit and strong does not mean that you are going to automatically win because the other person might be more experienced and have better technique than you, but having that strength, or positional power, will increase your chances of winning the fight. Here are the common positional powers:

Power of title. This type of power is your particular role or job title that you possess. It is directly connected with the people that you can influence and the decisions you can make that will affect the other side. If you are a manager for the clothing department, then you have a lot of power over the people in that particular department, but perhaps your positional power is not as powerful with the hardware department.

Power to punish. This is a very strong psychological power that can be best described as the ability to instill fear into the other side. Supervisors have the power to fire you from your job. A tough angry guy has the power to harm you for your actions. Police officers have the power to punish by writing you a citation or taking you to jail.

Power of reputation. This is your standing with your peers, community members, and workers. If you are well liked and received by everyone else, then this becomes a negotiating power for you. Being an expert or a well-known celebrity also increases your power of reputation. Good or bad publicity can shape the way your reputation is handled.

Power of physical appearance. Countless studies and psychological research has shown that appearance matters when dealing with people. The more attractive you are, the greater your positional power is. Attractiveness is not solely determined by your genetics however. Your hygiene, grooming, and clothing all count towards your level of physical appearance.

Power of resources. This is how much resources a person is able to call to their aid in a negotiation. Resources could be money, property, network contacts, or manpower.

Acquired Powers

Acquired powers are the negotiating powers that you create for yourself during the span of the negotiating process. Unlike positional power, you have full control over maximizing your acquired power to level the negotiating playing field. One of the added benefits is that acquired powers do not create conflict because they are being created from scratch at the negotiating table, rather than being brought in from the beginning. Here are the common acquired powers:

Power of your alternatives and options. Having several options and alternatives in a negotiation setting provides you with the independence to take your time and choose your best offer. Conversely, without such options, you will be forced into an easy submission by the other side. Having a plan B also gives you a baseline on the minimum amount that your are willing to accept in a negotiation, which also empowers you with the ability not to be taken blindly by your counterpart.

Power of flexibility. Being able to adapt and to change yourself to meet the specific demands of a particular person or situation is a huge power that you can acquire in a negotiation.

Power of rapport. Building rapport with your counterpart carries a lot of influential power along with it. Negotiations involve a final commitment and a commitment involves both parties trusting that the other will fulfill their end of that commitment. Build this power up by praising them, respecting them, making them feel comfortable and important, and listening to their concerns.

Power of patience. Having the ability to realize that a negotiation might take some time and having the patience to stay calm and not let your anger get the best of you throughout the process is a power.

Power of knowledge. Having knowledge about the company, product, issue, and your counterpart prior to dealing with them is a power. It allows you to influence them better and it protects you from being taken blindly.

Power of cooperation. By making your counterpart into a partner rather than an opponent and working together on the problem rather than fighting against each other is a great influential power. Cooperation facilitates problem solving and it creates a win/win situation.

Destiny

During a momentous battle, a general decided to attack even though his army was greatly outnumbered. He was confident they would win, but his men were filled with doubt. On the way to the battle, they stopped at a religious shrine. After praying with the men, the general took out a coin and said, "I shall now toss this coin. If it is heads, we shall win. If tails, we shall lose. Destiny will now reveal itself."

He threw the coin into the air and all watched intently as it landed. It was heads. The soldiers were so overjoyed and filled with confidence that they vigorously attacked the enemy and were victorious. After the battle, a lieutenant remarked to the general, "No one can change destiny."

"Quite right," the general replied as he showed the lieutenant the coin, which had heads on both sides.

In a negotiation setting, it is not how much power you have that really matters—it's how much the other side perceives your power level to be that matters. You could have very little negotiating power on your hands, but if you are able to create the illusion that you have more positional or acquired powers than you really do, then this will work for you. This illusion comes from your self-confidence and how you project that self-confidence out onto your counterpart. You might be a nobody, but you will remain a nobody if that is what you believe yourself to be. If you are a nobody, but you believe yourself to be a somebody, then you will rise up to be that somebody.

Befriend Time

In a negotiation, time is one of your most powerful weapons and a trusty ally by your side. By investing in time, you can allow your rational mind to do the negotiating instead of your emotional mind. Time also allows you to spot the other side's tactics and gives you the ability to counter those tactics with your own. Time also works to uncover the other side's interests and needs underneath their demands. Also the longer you are able to prolong the negotiation, the sooner the other side will feel the urge to close the deal. A negotiation is not s sprint to the finish line, it is a marathon and you need to be able to pace yourself and prepare for the long haul.

Deadlines

Time plays a crucial factor in a negotiation. There are two general truths about time in correlation with negotiation: (1) that 90% of all negotiations close in the last moments before a deadline and (2) the party with the *perception* of having more time on their hands has leverage. Deadlines precipitate action. This is because during the initial phases of a negotiation, there is plenty of time to throw around and there is very little incentive for the negotiating parties to take any action or make any concessions. However, when the deadline rolls near, the parties are more compelled to take action and the party who is more pressed for time will make the most concessions. This has always been one of the truths in negotiating—time is power. But its not just time that holds the power, it's the perception of having time on your hands that is the key here and this is why you can influence your counterpart into action by making them believe that you have more time on your hands than they do. Just remember that deadlines add pressure to a negotiation and it forces decision making.

In a negotiation, patience is always rewarded, especially when the other side springs something unexpected on you. In the case with telemarketer's, they try to employ ambush negotiating tactics on unwary consumers because they know that if they apply pressure on the consumer to make a decision now, they will be easier to influence because they won't have a chance to think it over and determine if it is good or fair. Avoid making any decisions on the quick, especially if someone else is presenting those options. A quick rule is to automatically default to telling them that you want to think it over and then disconnect.

Slow Down

It seems like so many things that are marketed in our society today rely on the premise that faster is better. While this might be true for pizza delivery, it means certain death in a negotiation setting. Handling a negotiation in a quick manner can be very risky and add being unprepared into that mix and you have a surefire way of being taken advantage of. Then why do so many people enter negotiations with this mindset? The answer to this mostly has to do with how our society programs us. We are taught at a very young age to get things done quickly and then move on to the next one, therefore, when the adult enters into a negotiation; their classical education has taught them that they also need to deal with that particular situation quickly. Marketing companies know this and bank off this by using marketing tools such as telemarketers to get the victim to make a decision right there on the spot. A Street Negotiator takes his time—as much time as is necessary to reach a fair agreement and push past all the deception and tactics that might be thrown his way initially. Remember that a negotiation is not like paying for airtime during the Super bowl. The only restriction you have is your level of patience with the situation and Street Negotiators are patient individuals who take as much time as is necessary to solve the problem. Slow down and use time to your advantage.

Gain Negotiating Leverage through Intelligence-Gathering

You should never enter a complex negotiation without preparing for it beforehand. You need to know as much information on the product, person, or company before you start negotiating with them so you won't be dealing blindly. Knowledge is a negotiating power that you can easily acquire more of and this entails some homework on your part. Remember that the more knowledge you are armed with before you enter a negotiation—the greater your overall chances of success will be.

Know Your Opponent before Stepping Into the Ring

Long before a professional boxer steps into the ring, you can be sure that he has spent many hours with his coach watching previous fights that his future opponent has been in so that he can dissect his technique, strengths, and weaknesses and use this knowledge to increase his own chances of success. Likewise, you will want to learn everything you can about the person you will be negotiating with before stepping into the negotiating ring so that you can understand their perspective better. Here are some strategies you can use:

- Gain information by talking with peers, friends, customers, employers, and coworkers.
- Reading their published work.
- Visit their website if they have one.
- Research local news articles on them.
- Do an Internet search on their name.

<u>Some topics to research on your negotiating counterpart</u>

- Playing style.
- Goals & Interests.
- Plan B.
- Level of Authority to make decisions.
- Background i.e. education, training, experience, values, etc.

Know Exactly Who You Should Be Negotiating With

It makes no sense to be negotiating with someone who does not have the authority to meet your needs. Save yourself the time and make sure beforehand that you are dealing with someone who has the authority to negotiate with you.

On that same token, make sure you do not automatically go over the head of the person that does have the power to negotiate with you. This is a common occurrence with unsatisfied customers in the service arena. They automatically shut themselves off from the subordinate and go straight to upper management. "I want to speak to the manager," is an overused phrase that often does more harm than good because it directly threatens the subordinate by telling them that they are incompetent and that now their boss will know how incompetent they are. It also works against you because the manager is usually less informed about the situation, usually sides with his subordinate, and is more concerned about managerial duties than the actual technical aspect of the problem that you are facing.

Make sure that the person you are dealing with has the power to negotiate with you and do not go over them just because anger and frustration kicks in.

Other Topics to Research

Price. If you are going to be making a large ticket purchase and will be dealing with a sales person, then you will want to research the fair market value for the item or property you are negotiating so that you can establish a fair standard. Use the Internet to search for competitor's prices and print out a copy of the lowest price you can find for the same item and take that with you when you negotiate. There are numerous paper and electronic publications out there for every product or service imaginable.

- What is the fair market price?
- What is the high and low price?
- What are the included "extras" that come with the price?
- What is the reliability of the product or service?
- What can they offer me that I can't get somewhere else?

Company or business. If you are going to be negotiating for a job, then you will want to be knowledgeable about the company you are planning on working for. Most companies and businesses these days have websites, so go search for their website and soak up all that useful information. Chances are that the interviewer will ask you some questions related to your knowledge of the company.

- What does the company do?

- What is their mission statement?
- Who are the top dogs of the company?
- What values are important to the company?
- What can I offer them that other people can't?

Subject matter. If you are negotiating the sale of a product or service then you want to be the foremost expert on that subject matter. Will you be discussing a particular field of interest or subject matter with the person you will be negotiating with? If the person likes a certain football team, then check what the current stats and recent news on that team is. If you will be going to a French or Japanese restaurant, it would be best to know how to pronounce some of the items on the menu and the proper etiquette for dining there.

- Relevant laws and legal material
- Cultural differences
- Etiquette
- Interests of the other party i.e. sports, movies, books etc.

Sources of Information

- Internet
- Library
- Universities / colleges
- Experts
- Books
- Magazines
- Videos
- Friends
- Family members
- Coworkers
- Employees
- Employers
- Trade journals
- Previous customers or clients
- Company publications

Where Should You Conduct Your Negotiation?

You have to take into consideration where you will be negotiating and the communication medium by which you will be exchanging ideas i.e. face-to-face, phone, e-mail etc. On whose court will the negotiation take place? Remember that in Street Negotiations, the goal is to facilitate cooperation, not create conflict or fear, so you want a place where both parties will feel comfortable.

Types of Communication Options

Face-to-face. Face-to-face communication is the best form of communication around because it is intuitive. Both parties are sending and receiving information at the same time and reacting to each other in real time. It also offers the largest pipeline of information exchange. In a face-to-face conversation, you can read their nonverbal language, avoid miscommunications, and get instantaneous feedback on their behavior and reactions. The downside is that face-to-face communication is not always possible or convenient in this fast-paced era to meet everyone in person. In addition to that, some other drawbacks are that you have to think on the spot, consider time as a factor, and pay attention to your own nonverbal signals as well. In some cases, such as a crisis negotiation, face-to-face communication might be too dangerous for a negotiator to choose.

Phone. Communication by phone has the advantage of being practical when you cannot visit in person and you have the added benefit of being able to have all your notes laid out in front of you that the other person can't see. Hence, you can be more prepared when going into a phone negotiation. You can also conduct talks in the comfort of your own home. The drawback is that you will not be able to see the other person's reactions or read their nonverbal behavior over the phone, so your vocal skills must be very good to compensate. Police negotiators always handle negotiations over the phone because they try never to put themselves in harms way and their track record speaks for the effectiveness of telecommunication. My only suggestion is not to handle important negotiations over the cell phone. Cell phones are too unpredictable in nature and you don't want a technical problem with cellular communication to ruin a perfectly good negotiation.

E-mail. This form of communication has its power in convenience. It gives you time to check correspondences at your own leisure and take your time in responding to them. The drawback of e-mail correspondence is that there is a lot of room for miscommunication, since written words are the only means of gauging emotional status. Due to the convenience, quickness, and inexpensiveness of e-mail, people often treat it as if they were talking face-to-face, but because of that room for the written word to be interpreted differently by the other person, e-mail is still a telegraph form of communication. There is an issue of privacy since e-mails are savable and there is no assurance of its confidentiality. Also it is less personable than talking to someone over the phone or in person and it is easier to disconnect yourself form that person through electronic correspondence. Email negotiations take lots of time, so if you are pressed for time, email may not be the best way.

Postal. Letters by mail are great for adding formal emphasis and importance to a negotiation. It shows the other person that you are not only professional, but serious as well. The downside to postal communication is that it's a slow process.

Video / web conferencing. If you are a techno-geek and know your way around the equipment then web conferencing can be a convenient and comfortable way of handling a meeting that would otherwise involve a lot of traveling, but if you are not good with computers and related web conferencing equipment, then skip this one because you don't want to be 4 minutes away from closing a good deal to run into equipment problems that you are not trained to fix. Another drawback of web conferencing is the lag-time associated with the transmission of data. There is usually a one to two second delay in sending video over the Internet and this can cause misinterpretations as to facial expressions and attitude.

Creative Alternatives to Office-Based Meetings

Negotiations are a highly dynamic process and while the problem might be similar, the person will always be different. Some might handle the office-based meeting quite well, but some might not like the stuff and boring nature of the office. You must decide based on the information that you have on the person where you will conduct the negotiation, but the options are limitless.

Negotiating in the playground. It's a funny thing—keep kids locked up inside the house and it can be near impossible to deal with them, but take them to the playground and their attitudes change immediately. We, as adults, have cast aside our slides and sandboxes and instead adopted golf courses, casinos, and poker rooms, and glitzy rooftop parties as our new playgrounds. What is nice about having negotiations in these places is that it lowers the person's defenses about dealing with you and it puts them in a good mood. It also establishes rapport and builds the relationship by getting them to see you as a friend more than a business person. Find out what kind of playground your other side enjoys, and see if he will talk with you on par 18 on a clear sunny day instead of stuck inside your office all day long.

Negotiate in a restaurant. Food is the universal symbol of happiness to every person in every culture because it fulfills one of our most basic and primal needs of survival—hence we unconsciously associate food with happiness. A negotiator can use the simple psychological law of association to make the restaurant negotiation work in his favor. The law of association says that a person will tend to associate the warm feelings that they are experiencing at the time with the person that they are with at that time. Food tends to make people feel happy and their happiness will be unconsciously associated with you.

Some Advice on Using Telephones

Get rid of call waiting. Nothing is more rude and annoying than someone who answers the phone then tells you that they will call you back "in a second" because they are on the other line and makes you wait for them to call back—which sometimes does not happen at all. Do yourself a favor and save yourself the money and don't subscribe to any call-waiting service, which includes your cell-phone. Not only is call-waiting disrespectful to the other person, but it also conveys to them that you have some kind of ego trip—that you are more important than they are or that you are some kind of "big shot." Instead, let them leave a message and call them back, or if it's important enough then they will call you back. Don't waste his or her time and avoid disrespecting anyone over the phone by simply getting rid of this obnoxious little service. You might even be saving a couple of bucks out of the deal.

Avoid using cell phones for negotiating. While cell phones have become an indispensable tool for on-the-go communication, these little gadgets should not be relied upon for negotiating. Cell phones are just too unreliable to be counted upon in an important negotiation. Since nonverbal communication is not a factor in phone conversations, the clarity of verbal communication over the phone is crucial. Miscommunication is just too commonplace in cell phone conversations to be an appropriate choice of communication for a negotiation.

Step II

<pre>
         P
Emotional Control
         R
         P
         O
         S
</pre>

"Speak when you are angry and you will make the best speech you will ever regret."

--Lawrence J. Peter

Worse than a Clown

There was a young monk who was eager to attain enlightenment. Once day, this monk came across something he did not understand, so he went to ask the master. When the master heard the question, he kept laughing. The master then stood up and walked away, still laughing.

The young monk was very disturbed by the master's reaction. For the next 3 days, he could not eat, sleep nor think properly. At the end of 3 days, he went back to the master and told the master how disturbed he had felt.

When the master heard this, he said, "Monk, do u know what your problem is? Your problem is that YOU ARE WORSE THAN A CLOWN!"

The monk was shocked to hear that, "Venerable Sir, how can you say such a thing?! How can I be worse than a clown?"

The master explained, "A clown enjoys seeing people laugh. You? You feel disturbed because another person laughed. Tell me, are you not worse than a clown?"

When the monk heard this, he began to laugh. He was enlightened.

What Causes Anger?

Anger is a strong emotion of displeasure caused by some type of grievance that is either real or perceived to be real by a person. The cognitive behavior theory attributes anger to several factors such as past experiences, behavior learned from others, genetic predispositions, and a lack of problem-solving ability. To put it more simply, anger is caused by a combination of two factors: an irrational perception of reality ("It has to be done my way") and a low frustration point ("It's my way or no way"). Anger is an internal reaction that is perceived to have an external cause. Angry people almost always blame their reactions on some person or some event, but rarely do they realize that the reason they are angry is because of their irrational perception of the world. Angry people have a certain perception and expectation of the world that they live in and when that reality does not meet their expectation of it, then they become angry.

It is important to understand that not all anger is unhealthy. Anger is one of our most primitive defense mechanisms that protects and motivates us from being dominated or manipulated by others. It gives us the added strength, courage, and motivation needed to combat injustice done against us or to others that we love. However, if anger is left uncontrolled and free to take over the mind and body at any time, then anger becomes destructive for the Street Negotiator.

Why Do We Really Care What They Say?

First of all, our anger is tied in with our level of self-esteem. We need to feel good about ourselves in order to maintain a sense of happiness and well-being. Therefore, when another person makes a crude comment to us, this attacks our perception of self-esteem and likewise, we are compelled to defend and attack in much the same manner as if we were assaulted physically. We care what they say because we fear that what they have to say will damage our self-esteem.

What is Egotism?

One day, during his usual visit, the Prime Minister asked the master, "Your Reverence, what is egotism?" The master's face turned red, and in a very condescending and insulting tone of voice, he shot back, "What kind of stupid question is that!?"

This unexpected response so shocked the Prime Minister that he became sullen and angry. The Zen master then smiled and said, "THIS, Your Excellency, is egotism."

Why We Need to Control Anger

Just like a person who is under the control of a street drug—a person under the influence of anger cannot rationalize, comprehend, or make good decisions because anger distorts logic into blind emotion. You become unable to think clearly and your emotions take control of your actions. Physiologically speaking, anger enacts the fight or flight response in our brain, which increases our blood pressure and releases adrenaline into our bloodstream, thereby increasing our strength and pain threshold. Anger makes us think of only two things: (1) Defend, or (2) Attack. Neither of these options facilitates a good negotiation.

Anger comes with a feeling of helplessness and a loss of control with external events. An angry person tries desperately to regain that control by exerting more aggression out on the external world, but they fail to realize that the world cannot change—that it is their own perception of that unchangeable world that needs to change. This inevitably leads the angry person into depression.

Self-Control

One day there was an earthquake that shook the entire Zen temple. Parts of it even collapsed. Many of the monks were terrified. When the earthquake stopped the teacher said, "Now you have had the opportunity to see how a Zen man behaves in a crisis situation. You may have noticed that I did not panic. I was quite aware of what was happening and what to do. I led you all to the kitchen, the strongest part of the temple. It was a good decision, because you see we have all survived without any injuries. However, despite my self-control and composure, I did feel a little bit tense - which you may have deduced from the fact that I drank a large glass of water, something I never do under ordinary circumstances."

One of the monks smiled, but didn't say anything.

"What are you laughing at?" asked the teacher.

"That wasn't water," the monk replied, "it was a large glass of soy sauce."

Sources of Anger

Physiological sources. The body has the ability to make us angry when we are physically attacked. An increase in physical pain diminishes our tolerance for anger, thus making it possible for us to become instantly angry when that pain threshold is crossed.

Cognitive sources. This is how we perceive the outside world to be. People whose anger comes from their cognitive source often perceive things as they should be, rather than how it actually is. They hold a certain expectation that their environment should follow and when it doesn't, their reality starts to fall apart.

Behavioral sources. This source of anger is a learned type of behavior that comes from the environment that the person creates for themselves through their experience and interactions with other people. For example, a young child who was punished for being dirty might later on associate dirtiness with anger.

True Self

A distraught man approached the Zen master. "Please, Master, I feel lost, desperate. I don't know who I am. Please, show me my true self!" But the teacher just looked away without responding. The man began to plead and beg, but still the master gave no reply. Finally giving up in frustration, the man turned to leave. At that moment the master called out to him by name. "Yes!" the man said as he spun back around. "There it is!" exclaimed the master.

Additional Internal Contributors to Anger

Emotional reasoning. People who tend to reason emotionally misinterpret normal events and things that other people say as being directly threatening to their needs and goals. People who use emotional reasoning tend to become irritated at something innocent that other people tell them because they perceive it as an attack on themselves. Emotional reasoning can lead to dysfunctional anger in the long run.

Low frustration tolerance. All of us, at some point, have experienced a time where our tolerance for frustration was low. Often stress-related anxiety lowers our tolerance for frustration and we begin to perceive normal things as threats to our well-being or threats to our ego.

Unreasonable expectations. When people make demands, they see things as how they should be and not as they really are. This increases their frustration tolerance because people who have unreasonable expectations expect people to act a certain way or for uncontrollable events to behave in a predictable manner. When these things do not go their way, then anger, frustration, and eventually depression set in.

People-labeling. People-labeling is an anger-causing type of thinking where the person applies a derogatory label on someone else. By rating someone as a "bitch" or a "bastard," it dehumanizes them and makes it easier for them to become angry at the person.

Recognizing the Signs and Symptoms of Anger

By recognizing the physiological signs of anger, we can attune ourselves to know when it is time to take measures to make sure that our level of anger does not get out of control. Here are some signs and symptoms of anger:

Physiological Symptoms

- Muscle tension.
- Teeth grinding.
- Increased breathing (both shallow and fast.)
- Feeling hot.
- Perspiration.
- Face turns pale.
- Sweating.
- Shaking in the hands.
- Dry mouth.
- Heart rate increases.
- Adrenaline is released into your system creating a surge of power.

Behavioral Symptoms

- Inability to sit still
- Difficulty sleeping
- Explosive outbursts, leading to physical attacks or destruction of property
- Rapid, negative, and unusually harsh responses to other people
- Social withdrawal
- Refusing to follow instructions or rules even if they are fair

- Use of passive-aggressive behavior
- Refusing to participate in an activity

Am I Right to be Angry?

Of course you are. You have your own perception and expectation of the world that you live in, and when the reality that you live in fails to meet your expectations, then yes you have the right to be angry. Afterall, if everyone thought alike, then the world would be a pretty dull place to live. You are going to run into situations that you don't enjoy. You are going to run into people who don't respect your views and ideas. The feeling of anger is totally justified according to your beliefs so don't repress or deny those feelings.

Having the right to feel angry does not mean that you have the right to lash out in anger by attacking the other person. You can't change the views of other people to conform to your own because, like you, they have their own right to uphold their view of the world. The best thing you can do is recognize your anger and focus it on the problem instead of your counterpart.

Factors That Lower Our Frustration Tolerance

Stress/Anxiety. When our stress-level increases, our tolerance for frustration decreases. This is why there are so many domestic disputes and divorces over financial problems.

Pain. Physical and emotional pain lowers our frustration tolerance. This is because we are so focused on taking care of our survival needs, that we do not have time for anything or anyone else.

Drugs / Alcohol. Drugs and alcohol affect how our brain processes information and can make a person more irritable, or bring forward repressed emotions or memories that can trigger anger.

Recent irritations. Recent irritations can also be called "having a bad day." It's the little irritations that add up during the course of the day that lower our tolerance for frustration. Recent irritations can be: stepping in a puddle, spilling coffee on your shirt, being late for work, being stuck in a traffic jam, having a flat tire.

The Spider

A Tibetan story tells of a meditation student who, while meditating in his room, believed he saw a spider descending in front of him. Each day the menacing creature returned, growing larger and larger each time. So frightened was the student, that he went to his teacher to report his dilemma. He said he planned to place a knife in his lap during meditation, so when the spider appeared he would kill it. The teacher advised him against this plan. Instead, he suggested, bring a piece of chalk to meditation, and when the spider appeared, mark an "X" on its belly. Then report back.

The student returned to his meditation. When the spider again appeared, he resisted the urge to attack it, and instead did just what the master suggested. When he later reported back to the master, the teacher told him to lift up his shirt and look at his own belly. There was the "X".

Rational Mind versus Emotional Mind

Anger is the biggest roadblock in a negotiation. When another person verbally attacks you, then instinctively your emotional mind, driven by your ego, comes into play and you react to their words without any thought. This "reaction" only breeds additional conflict however, so we need to explore better ways of controlling our anger.

It is important to understand that everyone has two different types of minds—the rational mind and the emotional mind. Whenever we involve ourselves in a negotiation of any kind, we always want to have our rational mind doing all the work because it processes information logically and objectively, weighing in all available information and selecting the best course of action for us. Our emotional mind, however, is not rational. It is primal in nature and ego driven. It makes poor decisions for us that are based on fixing an emotional need. This type of mind is dangerous for the negotiator to use because it is rash and unpredictable and almost always irrational.

Rational mind. The rational mind processes information objectively and weighs all possibilities and options for the given situation. The rational mind gathers all available information, processes it, and then generates a best possible response. The rational mind is objective and not attached to any emotion. It chooses the best options for any given situation. This is the mindset of the negotiator.

Emotional mind. The emotional mind is very quick to react to external stimuli, especially personal attacks. It is a need-based mind that seeks to take care of our emotional needs. The emotional mind can be very powerful and can easily overtake the rational mind in situations involving a lot of emotion. Even the brightest and smartest are not immune to being driven by the emotional mind. It is the reason why we do stupid things when we get angry or are in love, because our emotional mind takes control and starts driving our lives recklessly. Our emotional mind is instinctive. It has roots from our primal days where we needed to react rather than respond. The problem is that as we evolved, our emotional minds remained the same and did not necessarily help us in the society of laws and norms that we live in today. It still kicks in to save us from emotional hurt, but often that reaction is not the best suited towards achieving our means.

Your emotional mind does have its place in your life, but that place is not at the negotiation table. Constantly evaluate and check yourself to see which mind you are using at any given time. If you find yourself being driven by emotion, unable to think with a clear mind, and quick to react, then you are using your emotional mind and its time to step back and let your rational mind catch up and regain control. Remember that as human beings, we are no longer reaction machines like other animals. Our rational mind has the ability to control our emotional mind and keep it from destroying delicate negotiations. Make sure you are driving with that rational mind.

React = Lose

We're not at all different than animals when it comes to defending ourselves from attack. We are programmed to defend, attack, or run-away to eliminate the threat. The only difference between humans and our four-legged brethren is that we defend ourselves from both physical and emotional attacks. We react automatically to protect our egos just as we react to protect ourselves physically. *Reaction*, however, is the exact opposite of what we want to do in a negotiation, because we lose all control of the negotiation and it becomes a war that no one can win. Your counterpart will try to bait you into reacting emotionally because then he has total control over your actions. He will use personal attacks much like baited fishing lines, hoping that he will snag a reaction from you. Whenever you deal with any type of conflict, whether it is at home, at work, or on the streets, *NEVER* react out of emotion. Remember that a reaction from you is an automatic defeat and they've won without even negotiating. Don't make it that easy for them.

Three Ways We React

Reaction is what comes naturally when we get verbally attacked. We do it automatically like a programmed response without even thinking about it. This is because we allow our mouth and our body to be controlled by our emotional brain rather than our logical one. If someone verbally attacks you, then your first reaction is to insult back or become defensive. While this might feel like the right thing to do, it only proliferates and escalates the problem because the other person has baited you into playing their game—a game where you are bound to lose. By reacting, you are letting your emotions take control of your actions, rather than your rational mind having control over them. You never want your emotions to take over your body and mouth because it never does the right thing. Take a look at these three ways we react:

Defending. When someone attacks your ideas, a common reaction is to defend that idea by giving supporting arguments and digging into your position. What most people don't realize is that the minute you become defensive, you have already lost the war. This is because by being defensive you unwittingly make yourself a target for additional attacks. By being defensive you are never able to regain the ground that you lost because your energy is spent defending your ground rather than conquering new territory.

Example

- "Your plan will never work. There are too many problems with it"
- "What do you mean problems? There's no problem with it. It will work."

Counterattacking. When someone attacks you, the tendency is to attack them in "eye for an eye" fashion. This almost never works however, because it starts a vicious cycle of escalating attacks against one another that inevitably damages the relationship in the long run. When you counterattack your counterpart, he will have the need to escalate his attack against you and so on—back and forth—until someone gets hurt.

Example

- "What happened to you? You look terrible today."
- "You look like a crap too, so watch your mouth."

Giving In. Some people are more prone to giving into demands. Instead of fighting back, they choose rather to submit. This avoids the conflict, but it also makes you feel used and manipulated and it rewards the other side for their behavior. This is also not an acceptable reaction.

Example

- "C'mon. Try this for one week. It's free. Please. I just need one more signup to win my prize."
- "Okay."

Tactical Withdrawal and Regroup

When a person becomes overwhelmed by anger, they temporarily lose their rational thought process--in essence, they become temporarily insane, so it makes no sense to stay in that situation. The best solution therefore is a tactical withdrawal from the situation to allow the mind to regain control of those emotions and to calm down. The idea of a tactical withdrawal is that you save face during the dispute by having control over your emotions and knowing that it is better to lose the battle in order to win the war. This is harder than it appears because your anger will be competing for that control. Commit yourself to the tactical withdrawal by saying out loud that you need time to cool off. Give yourself ample time to regroup and then address the situation again at a later time.

Apply H.E.A.T. When Tactical Withdrawal Is Not an Option

Reaction is an automatic reflex that works similar to jerking your hand away after touching a hot mug. Responding is a thoughtful approach that uses your rational mind to consider options and the consequences to those options. Responding is the process of separating your emotions from the problem and addressing the conflict in a tactical and objective manner.

Keeping your rational mind in control is harder said than done. Reaction is what we are genetically programmed to do and in most cases, it is what we are also taught to do. Think about it—if someone makes an insulting remark to you then almost automatically you retort back with some defensive or insulting remark in like-fashion. You don't even have to think about it—it just happens naturally. What you must therefore train yourself to do is to hold back those reactions and allow your rational mind to speak, rather than your emotional one. Here are three steps to respond to a personal attack:

Hold your tongue. The quickest way to lose an argument and damage a relationship is to speak while being controlled by anger. Speaking while angry does not involve any thought—it's a form of instinctual reaction designed to either defend ourselves or attack the other person. Since speaking while angry is a difficult thing to control, the best method to allow your rational mind time to regain control is by not saying anything for at least 10 seconds. Depending on your level of anger, the amount of time could be several seconds to several hours. During this period of time, focus on your breathing. Studies have shown that our breathing becomes rapid and shallow when we are angry. Focus on regaining control of your anger by practicing on taking control of your breathing. Nothing good ever became of something that was said out of anger, so there really is no point in damaging future relationships even further by allowing your emotions to take over. While you are silent, focus on managing your self-talk. Your self-talk is the inner voice inside your head that is usually the reason why we get angrier than we should. When we get angry, our self-talk usually pushes us towards action by telling us how dare that person do such a thing to us, or that we should make them pay for what they have done. Instead, tell yourself that you can remain calm and keep your cool. Tell yourself that you have no need to prove yourself in this situation and that you are going to respond tactically to your anger rather than be controlled by it.

Encourage their criticism and ask for their advice. Often the best thing to do when faced with intense emotions is to walk away and put distance between yourself and the other person. For service persons such as police officers, social workers, and customer service personnel, this is not always a viable solution. A police officer cannot simply walk away from a situation because they are feeling angry. Without the ability to retreat and knowing that attack is not an option, the only recourse is to acknowledge their criticism. Tell yourself that you do not have all the answers and that you should allow someone else to give you their opinions no matter how stupid they might be. Even if they really are wrong, still encourage their input because by doing so you are actively defusing your own anger by reframing it into positive assertion. Empathetic responses are a way of acknowledging the other person's opinion, while not giving in or agreeing with it at the same time. By giving an empathetic response, you are telling the person that you understand their perspective and respect it. If someone tells you, "You people don't know what the hell you are doing," an empathetic response would be, "Yeah, I know how it can appear that way, but let me try to help you. I know we can work together on this." Another good empathetic response is, "I understand where you are coming from. Talk to me about that. I'm listening."

Address the problem, not the person. Most people out of anger accuse the other person of offensive behavior. Usually this takes the form of an attack and it only bring additional conflict to the party because now the other person has to defend themselves against you. Rather than accuse the person or change their behavior, instead address your feelings to them. Communicate your feelings by using "I" statements rather than "you" statements. This has the effect of letting the person know that you are angry, while at the same time, not directly accusing them of it. Since there is no direct attack against them, they will not be compelled to counterattack and it will open up a channel of communication between both of you.

Time-out. This is your fail-safe plan. If you feel that you cannot control the anger inside of you by any of the previous methods, then at least have the self-control to walk away and cool off and relax to regain your composure instead of attacking them and risk ruining a long-term relationship. Psychologists agree that retreating and having time to think things over is the best way to regain your composure when faced with anger. In a negotiation type setting, this might not always be a viable choice, but you should consider it as a fail-safe if your anger gets the best of you.

Be Careful Not To Label

When negotiating with difficult people who make us angry, it's all too common to label them as sub-humans by calling them derogatory terms. By dehumanizing them, we make it psychologically easier for ourselves to distance ourselves emotionally from the person. If you refer to Bob as the *Asshole*, even if not to him directly, then the next time you deal with Bob, you are not going to be dealing with Bob the person, but rather with an *Asshole*. Look back at our history and you will see that labeling individuals and groups of people was partly responsible for the deaths of millions of innocent people.

Recognizing and Accepting the Facts Of Life

The key to any type of conflict or negotiation is to remain calm. This can be the hardest part of any type of conflict resolution, especially if it deals with a loved one who deliberately tries to verbally abuse you. The important thing is to remain cool and collective. Remember that they are trying to get you angry so that you act out of emotion, thereby burning away any power you once had. Anytime you talk out of anger, you give up whatever power you once had in the negotiation and give that all to them. DON'T DO IT.

You can't win every fight. You can't change the world. And you can't change other people. Accept those truths and move on.

People make mistakes. You make mistakes. I make mistakes. Everyone makes mistakes. This is how we learn and why we are human. Recognize the fact that everyone is fallible from time to time.

Realize that anger affects your health more than anyone else. Anger lives in your mind alone and if not properly treated, can work like a cancer, destroying your life. Don't harbor anger and don't spread it to others. Deal with it effectively by venting.

Assertiveness Is Not Always the Best Substitute for Aggression

Most books and teachings condemn aggressive behavior in lieu of assertive behavior. Aggressive behavior is intimidating your counterpart. "Get out of my office." Assertive behavior is stating your demand in a polite, but firm way. "I can't get anything done while you're here. Maybe we can talk later." While assertive behavior is much better than aggressive behavior at avoiding direct confrontation, it does little to make the situation positive. In fact, assertive behavior can be even more harmful because the other person obeys out of politeness, but deep down inside, they have resentment towards you because they know it's a command, masked by politeness. Backstabbing behavior could be generated out assertiveness.

Instead of making assertive requests, use thought-provoking questions to guide them in the right direction. Ask for their advice instead of making assertive statements. Remember that statements, whether they are aggressive or assertive, are easy to attack and cause reaction because they are solid targets to focus on and just because the person doesn't counterattack does not mean that they are not experiencing resentment. Questions on the other hand offer no such target and are subject to interpretation, so use questions instead of assertations.

- Aggressive: "Get out. I'm busy."
- Assertive: "I'm busy right now. Maybe we can talk later."
- Question: "Would it be possible for us to talk later?"

- Aggressive: "Take out the trash or else."
- Assertive: "Do me a favor and take out the trash, please."
- Question: "Would it be possible for you to take out the trash before you left?"

The Eight-Worldly Winds

A well-known scholar had befriended a Zen master. One day, the scholar believed he had made a great cultivation in his understanding of enlightenment. He wrote a poem and had it delivered to the Zen master who lived across the river. The master read the poem out loud to his disciples.

"Unmoved by the eight worldly winds [gain, loss, honor, disgrace, praise, blame, happiness and pain], serenely I sit on the purplish gold terrace."

To this the master took his brush and scribbled the word 'fart' on the letter and had his disciple return the letter to his friend. The scholar became upset and went across the river to scold the master for being rude and unappreciative of his work. The master laughed as he replied, "My friend, you are no longer moved by the eight worldly winds, yet with one 'fart' you ran across the river like a rat."

Emotional control is by far the most important step in the conflict resolution process because like this story illustrates, we often know what is right, but when the situation presents itself, we often do the wrong thing. So the real question is whether we have truly learned the lesson in the first place? We can as scholars tell ourselves that being calm, rational, and collected is the best thing in any conflict situation, but how we actually handle it when we are engaged in that process is where the learning and understanding must happen. Like the scholar, merely writing fancy prose on a piece of paper does not constitute actual learning. Having the ability to control one's reactions when a conflict occurs is the true test of such learning.

Stress Management

Negotiating and managing conflict everyday is stressful. I'll be the first to tell you that negotiating, whether it is on the job or in your daily life is an emotionally draining process and it is just as important to tend to your emotional well-being after the negotiating process is over so that you stay psychologically healthy. Remember that you are no different in your needs than the people that you deal with on a daily basis and you need to address those needs before you can deal with others.

The Present Moment

A warrior was captured by his enemies and thrown into prison. That night he was unable to sleep because he feared that the next day he would be interrogated, tortured, and executed. Then the words of his Zen master came to him, "Tomorrow is not real. It is an illusion. The only reality is now." Heeding these words, the warrior became peaceful and fell asleep.

What is Stress?

Stress is the emotional, mental, and physiological changes that you experience when all of life's demands exceed your personal resources and your ability to meet them. Stress is one of those primitive survival instincts that kept us alive back in our caveman days. We can't avoid stress in our lives because it is programmed in us, but we can control stress and make it work for us.

Symptoms of Stress

Physiological Symptoms

- Stomach Aches or heartburn.
- Insomnia.
- Sweating.
- Uncontrollable twitching 'Tics'.
- Constant illness or colds.
- Chronic fatigue.
- Poor appetite (either too much or too little food.)
- Nausea.
- Diarrhea or constipation.
- Headaches.
- Impotence.
- Hyperventilation.
- Tightness in the chest area.
- Muscle aches or tension.

Emotional Symptoms

- Anger.
- Depression.
- Lack of concentration.
- Hopelessness.
- Increase / Decrease in libido.
- Crying.
- Low self-esteem.
- Lack of humor.
- Cynicism.

- Anxiety.
- Irritability.

<u>Behavioral Symptoms</u>

- Excessive alcohol consumption.
- Taking tranquilizers on a regular basis just to sleep.
- Excessive smoking.
- Excessive drinking of caffenated beverages (i.e. coffee, tea, soda etc.)
- Lack of personal hygiene.

Chronic Stress

Chronic stress should be seen as a serious disease, which if left untreated, can become terminal just like cancer. Stress releases the hormones cortisol and aldosterone into your bloodstream, which have the effect of suppressing your immune system and increasing your blood pressure.

<u>Here are some illnesses that stress can aggravate:</u>

- Cancer.
- Colds and flus.
- Migraines.
- High blood pressure.
- Heart disease
- Lowered fertility.
- Hair loss (alopecia areata.)
- Ulcers.
- Irritable bowel syndrome.
- Skin problems (acne, hives, psoriasis.)

What Are The Three Stages Of Stress?

Alarm stage. The initial confrontation with a stressor is similar to that of anger because our brain perceives a stressor as danger and it then activates our "flight or fight" response. This response is due to the release of specific stress hormones into the blood system: adrenaline, noradrenaline, and cortisol. Our reactions, strength, and senses become heightened. The heart beats faster and blood is redirected to the muscles. The lungs take in more oxygen, sweating increases, and pupils dilate. All these responses happen involuntarily because the "flight or fight" response is one of those primal survival programs left over from our primitive days.

Resistance stage. The brain senses that the initial danger is over and it prepares the body for a long period of stress. The spike in adrenaline decreases and hormones such as cortisol and aldosterone are released into the blood system. Cortisol increases blood-sugar levels and aldosterone raises blood pressure for circulatory functions.

Exhaustion. The body's supply of stress hormones is in limited supply and when those hormones deplete, then this is known as adrenal exhaustion. The purpose of the stress hormones is to elevate the body's performance in a dangerous situation to remove it from danger. It's a short-term function and is not well-equipped to handle long-term stress. When these hormones become depleted, the body becomes exhausted.

Relaxation Techniques to Reduce Stress

Aerobic exercise. Aerobic exercise is the single best thing you can do to remove stress from your mind and body. Go for a jog, go for a bike ride, hop on the stair-master machine at your gym and work up a sweat. You will not only be staying healthy and shedding calories, but you will also be shedding that excess stress and anxiety as well.

Deep breathing. This technique is used to expel stress from your body. First take a deep breath through your nose and fill your lungs to maximum capacity. Hold that breathe inside your lungs for three seconds. While holding that breath, imagine all your anger and stress pouring into your lungs and mixing with all that air you have inside. After the three seconds are up, exhale all the air from your lungs, along with the anger and stress that is mixed in with the air. Fully compress your diaphragm to get the residual air out of your lungs. Repeat this procedure twice more for a total of three repetitions.

Guided imagery relaxation. This technique is used to give your mind a mental vacation away from all the anger, stress, and drama that might be in front of you. It relies heavily on a good imagination, so you will have to delve deep into your creative side of your brain. First, think about what your personal paradise is. If you died and went to heaven, where would that heaven be? My personal "mind vacation" is being on a tropical island in total seclusion from the world. I am lying in a hammock between two palm trees on the beach, sipping some tropical drink, and listening to the waves crash down on the shore. Having your personal paradise in mind, close your eyes and imagine yourself being whisked away to that destination at lightning speed. While in your paradise, no stressful or angry thoughts or emotions can reach you. You are in total bliss. Concentrate on all the wonderful feelings that you get there i.e. the sounds of the waves, the warmth of the sun, the cool breeze running through your hair, etc. (refer to following page). Playing music or nature sounds will help create a more powerful sensation of realism.

Muscular relaxation. Use this to relax the tension that is building in your muscles because of anger or stress, and to burn off some of that emotional energy that is caused by those emotions. Start by flexing all of your muscles like you were doing a bodybuilding pose. Sometimes it is helpful and less obvious if you are in a busy area to grab onto an immovable object, like a railing or a post and just tense all of your muscles for a good five seconds. There should be a constant and good amount of tension on these muscle parts, focusing in particular on tensing your neck, back, and chest muscles. After the five seconds, slowly relax your muscles and you will find that you are able to achieve a higher degree of muscular relaxation by doing this exercise.

Punch a pillow. If you find yourself in a fit of rage, then rather than punching a hole in the nearest wall or getting arrested by punching a person, take your rage out by beating a firm pillow up. Pent up rage needs to be expelled immediately, so do it at some inanimate object that you don't have to worry about later.

Listen to music. If you find that a specific type of music calms you down, then pop in a CD and listen to it alone and let the music seep all that anger out of you.

Meditation. Buddhist monks have known for generations the power of meditation to calm the mind and focus one's thoughts. You don't have to subscribe to eastern religion to practice meditation however. Find a nice quiet place that is free from distractions and sit in a comfortable position. Close your eyes gently and then start the meditation process by breathing in through your nostrils and exhale through the mouth. Focus on the sensation of the breath and follow the air as it enters through your nostrils and into your lungs and then out through your mouth. Your breathing should be the only thing that you are thinking about. Nothing else matters. Initially, your mind might be chaotic and cluttered with many thoughts, but focus only on your breathing and resist any temptation to follow any thoughts that enter your mind.

Aromatherapy. Aromatic baths or use of vaporizers are a great way to reduce stress. A warm bath has the additional stress relieving effect of relaxing your muscles.

Other Creative Stress-Reducing Techniques

- Stomping on empty soda cans.
- Hitting a weight bag or punching bag.
- Yelling in a paper bag.
- Ripping newspapers.
- Skipping rocks into a lake or ocean.
- Taking a martial arts course.

- Going to the batting cages.
- Writing in a journal.
- Using a hand strengthener ball or device.
- Stretching.
- Massage.

Preventative Stress Maintenance

Eat right. Your body requires proper nutrition in order for it to be able to supply the muscles with energy and to make essential hormones necessary to cope with stress.

Do Consume

Plenty of water (8 glasses a day minimum)
Zinc and Magnesium rich foods (seafood, beans, grains)
Vitamin A and Folic acid rich foods (dark greens, orange juice)
Wholegrain breads, cereals
Fresh Fruit and Vegetables
Low-fat milk or soymilk

Avoid

- Caffeine
- Alcohol
- Sugar
- Salt
- Saturated fats
- Skipping Breakfast. (Breakfast helps maintain steady blood-sugar levels throughout the day.)

Stay fit. One of the best ways of relieving stress is through physical exertion. Stress and anxiety cause a lot of pent up energy inside your body that needs to be released. Any type of aerobic exercise is the best choice for releasing stress, but exercise in general is better than nothing at all. By maintaining a healthy body, you will have the physical stamina to handle long and stress-involving negotiations. You should strive for at least three 30-minute sessions a week.

Sleep. You need adequate sleep for the body to recharge and repair itself after a long day's work. Make sure you allow yourself enough time for an adequate amount of sleep (6-8 hours).

Smile. By smiling you not only appear more confident, sociable, and attractive to others, but it unconsciously makes you feel better too.

Studies have shown that smiling makes you more relaxed and calms you down when you are stressed.

Avoid stress-causing situations. If you can avoid a stress-causing situation, then do so. While some stress-causing situations are unavoidable, there is simply no reason to add additional stress to your mind and body if there is no reason to. Avoid adding any unwarranted stress to your life.

Step III

P
E
Reducing Tension
P
O
S

If you are patient in one moment of anger, you will escape a hundred days of sorrow

~Chinese Proverb

Nothing Exists

A young student believed that he had discovered enlightenment. Desiring to show his attainment, he said to his master: "The mind, and sentient beings, after all, do not exist. The true nature of phenomena is emptiness. There is no realization, no delusion, no sage, no mediocrity. There is no giving and nothing to be received."

The Zen master, who was smoking quietly, said nothing. Suddenly he whacked the student with his bamboo pipe. This made the youth quite angry.

"If nothing exists," inquired the master, "where did this anger come from?"

Reduce Tension with Active Listening Skills

Active listening is a way of listening and communicating with another person in an effort to increase understanding. Active listening also has the added benefits of establishing rapport and cooperation by creating empathy. Active listening seeks not only to understand the ideas of the person, but also to uncover information about their interests, beliefs, and what is important to them. Active listening is your way of collecting information on that person. You want that information to flow freely from their lips and you want that information to be as accurate as possible. Active Listen is comprised of five parts.

Why Actively Listen?

To be able to effectively gain the compliance of your counterpart, you are going to have to know how they see the situation. No two people ever see the same situation in exactly the same way. There could be house that is on fire and person A will be worrying about the people who might be inside, person B might be worrying about the animals inside, and person C might be worrying about his house being next door. All three people see the same thing—the burning house, but not all three people are thinking the same thing about that burning house. The same hold true for a negotiation. You and your counterpart might share a similar problem, such as a car accident, but you might be worried about getting to work on time for an important meeting, while the other person is worried about waiting for a police report. Clearly, the car accident is a shared problem between you both, but the interests are different. Never assume what the interests of the other person are because that leads to conflict. Instead, listen to them talk and be able to pick up on what their interests and needs are while they are talking.

Keeping Silent

Four monks decided to meditate silently without speaking for two weeks. By nightfall on the first day, the candle began to flicker and then went out. The first monk said, "Oh, no! The candle is out." The second monk said, "Aren't we not suppose to talk?" The third monk said, "Why must you two break the silence?" The fourth monk laughed and said, "Ha! I'm the only one who didn't speak."

What Are Burning Issues?

Burning issues are the pressing issues and concerns that a person is experiencing that cloud their ability to make long-term judgments. People generally need to vent these burning issues out more than anything, with the implicit requirement that the other person listens and acknowledges what they have to say. Usually, the venting person is not seeking any type of advice or help on these issues, but they just have the need to get them off their chest. What generally happens in a conflict setting, however, is that the other party is talking and trying to get their own burning issues off their chest. When both parties are talking, that means that none of them are listening and hence, none of them are getting their implicit needs of having the other person listen and acknowledge their concerns because they are both yapping away. The key to reducing tension is to use active listening to defuse and eliminate those burning issues and clear them off the path towards agreement.

The Importance of Active Listening During a Negotiation

Uncovers interests. Interests are the focus of the negotiation and uncovering them is part of your goal. Listening to the concerns of your counterpart, will make those interests stand out and be easier for you to identify. Keep in mind that if they want to express their concerns, then that means they are giving you free information that you won't have to ask for later in the game.

Reduces miscommunication. A lot of unnecessary conflict happens because we misinterpret someone's meanings. Active listening reduces the chance of miscommunication by being able to confirm the information that you received from them by paraphrasing and gives them the opportunity to correct your information if it is wrong.

Reduces anger. The best negotiator in the world can't persuade someone who is controlled by hostile emotion. To bring them back to the table, you have to disarm their anger first. Active listening provides an excellent vent to release that pent up anger. It allows your counterpart to voice their concerns and it fulfills their need for someone to listen and empathize with their situation.

Makes them a better listener. Since active listening involves you paraphrasing their story back to them, it automatically forces them to become active listeners themselves. Everyone is curious to hear their words through the mouth of another person and so they will give you their undivided attention while you are talking. They must actively process the information spoken to them in order to correct any misinformation that you might say.

Builds rapport. Active listening builds rapport through empathy. By listening to their concerns and actively engaging them in conversation, you will be giving them the unconscious message that you are interested in what they have to say and that you understand where they are coming from.

Increases persuasion. Active listening makes them trust you more because you have dedicated your time to listening and addressing their concerns. The psychological rule of reciprocity will persuade them to return that favor.

The Four Steps to Active Listening

1. **Listening & understanding.** You are listening to the words spoken to you and reading your counterpart's nonverbal commu-

nication to get a good picture of what they are thinking. Listening is not just hearing, but also internalizing and understanding what is being spoken to you. For example, you can be listening to a Brazilian person speaking Portuguese, but if you do not understand Portuguese yourself, then you are not understanding what is being said. However, if the Brazilian person is also pointing to his wrist, saying "tempo?" while looking over to your watch, then you can probably assume that he is asking for the time. Listening requires all your senses to observe the person and take in as much information from them to understand what they are saying.

2. **Empathizing.** Empathy is the process of understanding an issue from the perspective of your counterpart. Metaphorically it can be likened to the saying, "walking around in another man's shoes" because you are trying to see things through the filter of their life and experiences rather than your own. This is important to gaining rapport and building trust with that person.

3. **Asking & encouraging.** By asking questions, you will be able to direct their focus onto key issues and also increase your charisma with them by seeking their opinions. Encouraging means you are letting the other person know that you are interested in what they have to say. Feedback is important to the other person because they have a need to know that their "faxes" are being received, metaphorically speaking. This is the process of getting the person to elaborate more on an idea so that you can paint a fuller picture of his frame of mind.

4. **Paraphrasing / Summarizing.** Paraphrasing is the skill of repeating back the other person's meaning with your own words. This is important in the active listening process because it prevents miscommunication and it also lets the other person know that you are understanding what they are telling you and that you are trying to empathize with them.

Listening and Understanding

When you are collecting information in the form of spoken words and body language from your counterpart; it becomes important that you internalize and process all their coded information so that you can translate it correctly. It's a lot like sending a picture to a friend through the Internet—things have to be sent and received correctly in order for the picture to look the same on both computers, but as we all know, things can go wrong in the transmission process, causing the picture to be uninterpretable by the receiving computer. Likewise, you want to make sure you download all your counterpart's information correctly and to do that you need to avoid certain things. When you are using your listen skills, avoid distractions, avoid thinking about other things, and avoid half-listening. These pitfalls of listening will only make the words go in one ear and right out the other. Remember also that when you are talking, you are not listening, so allow your counterpart to speak their mind and listen attentively. Learn how to read and interpret body language because that is a powerful supplement to understanding the spoken word and as I stated in the previous chapter, nonverbal communication is just as important as the spoken word when it comes to communication.

Give them your undivided attention. We all know how rude it is when you are having an important conversation with someone and their cell phone goes off and they answer it. It gives the talker the impression that you are hearing the words, but you are not listening. Active listening is like reading a book, knowing that you are going to have to do a book report afterwards, you need to give it your undivided attention and make notes either on paper or in your mind about the important points. Remember that you are going to have to paraphrase their story back to them later on, so give them your undivided attention and reduce distractions as best as possible.

Send nonverbal cues of interest. It is not enough just to listen to what the other side says—you have to show them that you are interested by sending nonverbal messages of enthusiasm. If someone were expressing something important to you, do you think they would appreciate talking to your back or your front? You have to send them a nonverbal message that lets them know that you consider their time important.

- **Eye contact.** Maintain good eye-contact throughout the conversation. This will tell them that your focus is on them and nothing else.
- **Body position.** People aim their upper torso in the direction of people who they are interested in, so position your body so that it aims directly at them. Be aware that your head can be facing them, but your body can be facing another direction. Make sure that your body is facing them too.
- **Posture.** Send the message that you are interested in what they have to say by leaning forward, either in your chair or standing up.
- **Smile.** Smiling is a universal gesture of acceptance and it makes the person feel comfortable expressing their concerns with you.

Be on the lookout for interests. Throughout your conversation, you want to keep your mind ready to pick out the motivating factors that guide the person's behavior. What is causing them to behave the way that they are? Chances are that they will vent this to you on their own, so keep your ear trained for these underlying issues

Show them that you understand. Whenever you engage in a conversation, the other side will have doubts on whether or not you understand them; therefore, feedback becomes an important factor in the listening process. You want to make sure that they know you are understanding their words by giving them verbal and nonverbal signs of understanding. Take a look at the following:

Examples of acknowledging words

- "HmmmHmmm."
- "I see."
- "I understand."

- "Gotcha."
- "Wow."
- "Ok."
- "Right."
- "Yeah."
- "You don't say."

<u>Examples of nonverbal cues of acknowledgement</u>

- "Hahahaha." (after something funny)
- Head nodding
- Looking into their eyes
- Smiling when they pause
- Changing your facial expression

Empathize To Gain Perspective

Empathy is the power to see something from your counterpart's point of view. Essentially it means to "walk in another man's shoes." Empathy is important in active listening because you want to see their ideas and their view of the problem through the lens of their mind—not yours. By empathizing with them you will not only absorb a lot of confrontation between you and your counterpart, but you will also gain valuable insight on how you can tackle a common problem together.

Empathy is your ability to step inside the shoes of your counterpart and walk around in them for a while and see things from their perspective. When you are using empathy, you try to understand the situation based on what you know of the person's history, background, experience, personality, and interests. By doing this you will have effactually crossed over and focused on the same problem together instead of being at odds with each other.

Ask yourself where this person has been. What places has this person been to that might shape his perspective? Has this person lived in one place his entire life? Has this person traveled the world? Has this person spent time in the military? How about time in jail or prison? The places one has been to will shape the way he see the world, so you must ask yourself where this person has been in his life.

Ask yourself who this person is. What kind of person is this guy? What does he do for a living? What is his education? What do you know of his family life? Our personality shapes the way we see the world, so you want to know who this person is.

Ask yourself what drives this person. What is this person's motivating factors? What drives him to do what he does? Profilers and detectives try to understand the logic behind serial killer's motives and beneath their twisted thinking there is some predictable logic to their motives. The problem is just figuring out what motivates them.

Ask yourself how you would have felt in the same situation. You need to try to understand the feelings and emotions the person is dealing with by asking yourself how you would have felt in the same situation. If someone is really excited about telling you his vacation stories, then you have to imagine how excited you would be coming back home from such an adventure.

Empathetic responses. These are the things that you say that let the person know you are trying to understand him from his perspective. Paraphrasing falls under empathetic speech, because you are spitting back his meaning with your words. With empathetic speech, you are relaying your perception of how he feels. Empathetic speech is powerful because, like paraphrasing, it shows the person that you are trying to understand his perspective, rather than exerting your own.

<u>Examples of Empathetic Statements</u>

- "I understand that you might feel angry because of…"
- "It seems like you feel depressed because…"
- "I sense that you are feeling angry."
- "I'm feeling that you are pretty angry at me right now."
- "I understand. That would make me feel bad too."

Strategies for Using Empathy

Acknowledge their ideas. You might not agree with their ideas—in fact, you might be dead set against them. A police detective definitely does not agree with a killer's motives, but he can still recognize the killer's motives as one reason out of many to commit such as crime. Statements such as "I understand where you are coming from." "I know what you mean." Tell the person that you acknowledge his ideas.

Acknowledge their emotions. Emotions are powerful factors in a negotiation and need to be acknowledged just as much as the person and his ideas. People who are dealing with some emotional concerns need someone to relate to what they are feeling. By acknowledging their emotions, you fulfill their need for someone who can relate to them. After the person expresses how he is feeling, tell him that you would feel the same way if you were in his shoes.

Don't psychoanalyze them. Unless you have a Ph.D. in psychology, it is best not to tell them how they are feeling, or why they feel that way because this will cause the other person to become defensive. No one likes to be told how he thinks or why he thinks that way, so you will inevitably cause conflict by making these assumptions. Instead relate to him how you think he feels and ask him to express to you the reasons behind that feeling.

<u>Examples</u>

- **Bad empathetic statement:** "You are angry because you failed your test."
- **Better empathetic statement:** "You seem angry today. Want to talk about it?"

- **Bad empathic statement:** "You are depressed because he dumped you."
- **Better empathetic statement:** "You seem sad to me. Did something happen recently?"

Don't confuse empathy with sympathy. It's important that you don't confuse empathy with sympathy because they are two different things. When you empathize with someone, you are seeing things from his perspective, from his "shoes." When you empathize, you attempt to understand them, but it does not mean you have to agree with them or even like them at all. When you sympathize with someone, you are taking pity on them and it affects your own judgment. Hostage negotiators are trained in the aspects of Stockholm Syndrome in which the actual hostages, over time, begin to sympathize with the hostage taker and may even work against the police who are trying to rescue them in the first place. Just remember that empathy is understanding. Sympathy is having pity.

Relate your own experience. A lot of times when you tell someone that you understand, they will lash back at you by telling you that you don't understand what they are going through. A way around this is to relate a personal story to them that mirrors what they are going through. By relating a personal experience to their own, you will show them that you do know what they are going through and that you may hold some valuable answers as how to deal with the situation.

Asking Questions and Encouraging Communication

Asking questions gently probes for interests and keeps the other side focused on what is important. Remember that the primary objective of active listening, besides reducing tension is to collect information about the other side's concerns—concerns that they might not be so willing to give up if they thought you were the enemy. Another positive benefit of questions, as we will find out later is that questions offer little to no target for attack. Questions are fluid like water rather than concrete like statements. When you offer a question, it makes the other side think rather than react. This aids in reducing tension. Also encouraging them to continue is important. Give open-ended questions and reward them for their responses with praise. Questions pertaining to their goals, beliefs, values, and opinions are very useful to generate participation. You want them to talk and give you information so you can uncover their interests, so always encourage their participation.

Get them to continue talking. Persuade them to keep talking to you by asking them to build on their story. Express interest in what they have to say.

Common Encouraging Words:

- "Go on"
- "Please continue."
- "Do tell."
- "Talk to me. I'm listening."
- "Talk to me about that."
- "I want to hear all about that."

Repeat the last word to encouraging more talk. A useful way to elicit more conversation out of the person is to simply repeat the last word or two that they said in the form of a question. We repeat the other person's last words naturally when we want clarification on it, but you can use it to your advantage when trying to encourage more conversation.

Examples

- **Them:** "I was really busy."
- **You:** "Busy?"

- **Them:** "I'm tired."
- **You:** "Tired?"

- **Them:** "I don't feel good."
- **You:** "You don't feel good?"

Using silence to encourage conversation. Silence is a powerful tool to encourage conversation. A common human behavior is to feel uncomfortable with periods of silence during a conversation. Silence encourages a person to talk and you can use this to your advantage during a conversation. Pose a question to them and let them think about it for awhile. Resist your own temptation to break the uncomfortable silence and let them think about an answer.

Use the law of reciprocity. Tell them a secret about you in order to enact the law of reciprocity. They will be more obligated to share a secret of theirs after you share one of your own. It also builds trust up because you have opened yourself up to them.

Let them know that you don't judge them by their actions. Let them know that you don't care what they did and that you don't judge them for their actions or behavior. Let them know that you have done some things in your life that you were not proud of or that got you in trouble and that you understand how they feel about it.

Give them incentive to talk to you. Make sure the person knows that he will benefit from talking to you. I usually tell someone, "I want to help you out here, but I need to know more about what happened." Some detectives I know use the line, "If you tell me exactly what happened, I'll do my best to help you out."

Focus on their feelings, not on the action. Ask them general questions about how they feel or how they felt when the incident occurred rather than what they did. This switches their focus away from being defensive and onto their need to express their feelings to someone. This is a particularly effective technique because it creates a strong bond of empathy between you and this generates more trust and forces him to open up to you.

Getting past "I don't know" answers. One of the most frustrating times during a conversation is when you are attempting to encourage conversation only to be shut down with annoyingly vague and apathetic answers like:

- "Nothing."

- "I don't know."
- "I just don't, Ok?"

Apathetic answers like these are given because they involve little or no thought on their part, or they feel guilty about their feelings and prefer not to want to spend the emotional costs of reliving them. Apathetic answers are usually given after vague questions are given such as:

- "How come?"
- "Why?"
- "What do you mean?"

The solution to getting past apathetic answers is to ask *specific clarifying questions* related to the topic that will make them feel obligated to respond with a more specific answer. Or if you think that they might not know how to answer the question, then ask them *how they feel* about the problem.

Paraphrasing

Paraphrasing allows you to confirm with the other person that you have interpreted his words and nonverbal communication into an accurate copy of his original idea. Paraphrasing ensures that there is no miscommunication between the two of you by periodically going back and confirming the correctness of your understanding. Paraphrasing also has the added benefit of letting your counterpart know that you are making an effort to understand him. It also hooks them into being an active listener themselves because they want to make sure that you have their ideas straight and if there are any inconsistencies with your version of their idea, then they can correct you.

Effective paraphrasing. Let them know that it's your interpretation. People don't like having words put in their mouths, especially if they are adamant that they never said those things. Cognitive psychologists have told me that the human memory has a tendency to mix actual facts with our own feelings and imagined visualizations, making our memory slightly different than the true reality. This is also true when people are speaking, because often we are so focused on certain thoughts while speaking, that we just assume that we expressed all the details of those thoughts, when in fact we might not have explained them well at all. Both of these memory flaws can cause a problem with miscommunication, which is why you should avoid telling them what they said exactly and instead put out a disclaimer that you are going to repeat what you have understood them to have said. This tells them that you are going to try to explain back to them their meaning as best you can, but it may not be totally correct. Take a look at these examples:

- "So, let me see if I understand you…"
- "Ok, so what you are telling me is…"
- "Correct me if I'm wrong…"
- "Tell me if I got you right here…"
- "What I'm hearing from you is…"
- "So, it seems to me that…."

Don't be a parrot. Paraphrasing does not mean you should be like a parrot and repeat every word that they say right back to them. Parroting someone will only make them upset because it will sound like you are patronizing them. Effective paraphrasing means you are taking their words and expressing their meaning with your own words.

Ask for corrections. Part of the beauty of paraphrasing is that it allows you to fully understand their key points and it makes them into a listener too because they are eager to hear what they said through your mouth. Ask them to correct your interpretation by saying, "Correct me if I'm wrong." Or attach the word, "Right?" at the end of the sentence. This will give them the opportunity to make changes in your statement, or make additions to their previous statements.

Ask for clarification. While paraphrasing, you might encounter certain portions of your counterpart's story that you don't understand, or gaps in the story that you need filled in. This is the time where you can ask for clarification on the information that is unclear.

- What do you mean by that?
- Can you tell me what happened after that?
- Who are you referring to?

Dealing with Personal Attacks

Throughout the active listening process, the other side will be trying to goad you into a verbal fist-fight to get you to play his game. Recognize this as a tactic and don't play into his game. Personal attacks are just the same as a fisherman casting out a baited line into the lake. You are the fish. Once you take the bait then the game is over for you. You become tonight's supper. Instead work around those personal attacks. Reframe them into opportunities for discussion. Remain professional. Let the fisherman know that you are too smart to take his bait and he will eventually give up. Use the following strategies to overcome verbal attacks.

Gift of Insults

There once lived a great warrior. Though quite old, he still was able to defeat any challenger. His reputation extended far and wide throughout the land and many students gathered to study under him.

One day an infamous young warrior arrived at the village. He was determined to be the first man to defeat the great master. Along with his strength, he had an uncanny ability to spot and exploit any weakness in an opponent. He would wait for his opponent to make the first move, thus revealing a weakness, and then would strike with merciless force and lightning speed. No one had ever lasted with him in a match beyond the first move.

Much against the advice of his concerned students, the old master gladly accepted the young warrior's challenge. As the two squared off for battle, the young warrior began to hurl insults at the old master. He threw dirt and spit in his face. For hours he verbally assaulted him with every curse and insult known to mankind. But the old warrior merely stood there motionless and calm. Finally, the young warrior exhausted himself. Knowing he was defeated, he left feeling shamed.

Somewhat disappointed that he did not fight the insolent youth, the students gathered around the old master and questioned him. "How could you endure such an indignity? How did you drive him away?"

"If someone comes to give you a gift and you do not receive it," the master replied, "to whom does the gift belong?"

Like the young fighter, your counterpart might try to goad you into making the first move by using verbal attacks, threats, and incredible demands. They want to expose your weakness so that they can exploit it mercilessly. The old warrior knew what his own weaknesses were and he knew better than to give up those weaknesses by making the first move out of anger over simple words. With any type of conflict you encounter, this will always be a common tactic of the other side. They will bait you with personal assaults to get you to play their game and expose your weaknesses. As the old warrior told his pupils, simply choose not to accept their gifts, or in our case verbal assaults, and then those gifts belong to no one.

Defeat the desire to win every fight. People have a natural tendency to want to win every argument that comes their way, no matter how trivial it might be. This is because we often allow our egos and face-saving to come into play. Domestic related murders have occurred over things as trivial as time spent on the Internet or whose turn it was to take out the trash. We have been classically conditioned to believe that the only way we can save face is by putting up an argument, by rejecting the other side's ideas and forcefully exerting our own. This of course does nothing but breed conflict. When dealing with other people in a conflict setting, know who is handling the conversation—you or your ego.

Ignore it and move forward. One of the simplest and most effective tactics to use when dealing with personal attacks is to ignore the attack and move forward, without ever acknowledging that the attack took place. Let it fall on deaf ears. This is effective particularly when the other side is making blanket threats and ultimatums to you, because you are not rejecting or challenging their threat and it allows you to test the seriousness of their threat. If they repeat their threats, then they might be serious, but if they don't bring it up again then it was a bluff.

Acknowledge their point and ask for their advice. When the other side makes an attack, it usually comes as a double-punch. First they attack your idea about how the situation should be handled and then they attack you personally. "That's a stupid idea. Can't you think of something better?" Resist the temptation to counterattack or defend yourself. Instead, acknowledge their point and ask them for advice. "Maybe you're right. What do you suggest?" What this effectively does is places it back on their shoulders to come up with a better solution than the one you presented. If they can't come up with one, then they end up looking like the idiot.

Don't make statements, use questions to make your point. Using statements will always get you into trouble when dealing with personal attacks. This is because statements take a hard-line stance on an issue and therefore become something that is concrete and easily to attack. Statements cause conflict because they back the person up against a wall and they have only two choices—go through your open door or go through you. Like a cornered animal, they will perceive your open door as a trap and take their chances going through you instead to get out. Questions on the other hand offer little or no resistance to attack. Questions are like water—they can crash with tremendous force and yet are shapeless and immune to attack. Questions can achieve the same objective as statements, but instead of being black or white, yes or no, questions direct the other person by educating them as to what their options are. Questions engage the mind and make them think about their available options, whereas, statements restricts options and usually falls on deaf ears.

Invite their criticism, rather than waiting for it. In many conflict situations, the typical exchange is that you pose an idea, the other side rejects that idea, you defend your idea, the other side attacks both you and your idea, you counterattack them back, and so on. You can effectively stop this from happening before it starts by simply inviting their criticism of your idea at the very beginning. "This is what I think. What do you think about this idea?" "Here's my idea, but I'm open to suggestions."

By inviting criticism at the onset of a proposition, you effectively change a criticism from being combative, into one that is cooperative. The ideas will be the same, but you will have the home-court advantage because they will be playing your game.

Use silence. In a conflict, there is a lot of bickering and sniping that goes on because both sides want to get their point across, but neither one of them is listening or acknowledging the other side. Instead, use the power of silence as your weapon against personal attacks or ridiculous demands. Silence is a powerful psychological tactic because it makes a good majority of people uncomfortable. Human behavior suggests that people will move away from being uncomfortable and towards something that is more comfortable. In this case, the person will think hard about something to say in order to get away from the silence and re-establish conversation. Silence also causes self-doubt. People who make incredible demands will start doubting themselves and their demands with silence because it takes on the characteristics of a false stalemate or impasse. You can also combine the effects of question-asking along with silence to get them to really generate some ideas. This works well when someone gives you a lame answer like, "I don't know." Rather than try to pry information out of them, which usually makes them defensive, instead resist the urge to say anything and give them silence instead. You will find that in a good majority of cases, the person will start elaborating on that answer as their solution to get away from the uncomfortableness of silence.

Avoid "*you*" statements, use "*we*" instead. Starting off a statement with *you* is almost always accompanied with some sort of criticism attached to it such as, *"You never take out the trash."* *You* statements are accusatory in nature. It invites conflict to happen. *You* statements signal to the other person that a criticism is coming their way and they prepare for it by becoming defensive and getting ready to counterattack. Instead, replace you statements with *we* statements. *We* statements suggest to the other side that you are on the same team rather than opponents. *We* statements are more difficult to attack because by attacking a we statement, they will in effect, be attacking themselves as well. Also by making a *we* statement, it neutralizes the harsh accusatory nature of the statement because the counterpart knows that the statement applies to both of you, rather than just to him.

Refer to the problem using "I" statements. When describing the nature of a problem, it becomes all too easy to criticize or attack the other side for what we perceive they did wrong to cause the problem. Obviously, this will result in their defensive action and counterattack. Instead, when describing a problem, refer to its impact on you personally, rather than focusing in on the actions of the other side. By referring to yourself, you are not provoking a conflict and you effectively remove the incentive for the other side to fight you.

Don't blame, focus on the future. People have the propensity to attach blame for past mistakes. Neither person wants to be blamed and criticized for a mistake and even if it was their fault, they don't want to be criticized for their mistakes because that only breeds hostility and resistance to the objective of reaching an agreement. Blaming your counterpart locks the both of you in the past, where nothing new can be accomplished. Instead, reframe that blame into an educational lesson on what can be done in the future. Living in the past will hinder any real growth from happening.

Give them the illusion of control. It's sometimes the case when the act of asking someone to do something will result in defensive or aggressive behavior. This is usually the result of the person's perception that you are trying to control their actions. Their fear of losing independence comes forward and they retaliate with anger to exert the fact that they are in control of their lives, not you. "Can you wash the dishes," "Can you sit down now," "Can you calm down," are prime examples of commands under the guise of questions. Be careful when you use command-questions because they can often set off an angry person. Instead, use a simple linguistic trick of rewording that question to make it seem less like you are giving a command and more like you are asking them for a favor. "I don't mind if you don't want to do the dishes," "I don't mind if you want to shout at me." The subtle linguistic change in wording does two things (1) it puts them in control of their own actions, and (2) it makes a subtle request as to what action you would like them to do. So if you are afraid of offending the person, then give them the illusion of control.

Use softening words to pad harsh statements. Softeners are words inserted into a commanding or demanding statement to "soften" it up and not make it so harsh-sounding. Some common softeners are: perhaps, maybe, I think, It's possible etc. Softeners take the roughness out of a harsh statement that might otherwise anger your counterpart. What makes softeners work is that they are subject to interpretation by your counterpart instead of being rigidly defined. Softeners allow you to introduce an opinion without sounding overbearing or pushy. Learning how to use softeners effectively is one of the best conflict-preventing tools you can have.

Most common softening words used

- Might.
- Maybe.
- Possible.
- Could be.
- Probably.
- Often.
- Mostly.
- At times.
- Hopefully.
- Occasionally.
- Usually.
- Rarely.
- I believe.
- I think.
- I like.
- I feel.
- I thought.
- I've experienced.
- I trust.

Specific Examples:

- **Harsh:** Go get your laundry out of the dryer.
- **Softer:** I think you <u>might</u> have laundry in the dryer and I need to use it.

- **Harsh:** I'm never wrong with that.
- **Softer:** I usually do that right, but <u>it's possible</u> that I made an error.

- **Harsh:** What do you know about that?
- **Softer:** <u>Maybe</u> you can explain that to me so I understand you better

- **Harsh:** You never do it right.
- **Softer:** <u>Maybe</u> we can work on this together to do a better job.

Step IV

P
E
R
Persuade
O
S

Focus their attention away from you and onto the problem—this is the essence of fighting without fighting.

~Tristan Loo

The Arguing Monks

Two monks became involved in a debate over the meaning of life. They argued the entire day over who was right. After not resolving the argument, they decided to go visit their master to settle the debate once and for all. They asked the master who was correct.

"You are correct." Said the master to the monk who had asked him the question. The first monk was ecstatic and left the room.

The second monk was angry and demanded to know why the first monk was correct. The master simply replied, "But you are also correct." Upon hearing this, the second monk ran from the room with delight.

A third monk who was watering the plants inside the master's room at the time the two monks had entered became very puzzled over the master's answer. Overwhelmed with curiosity, the third monk asked the master, "How can both monks be correct when their positions are completely opposite of each others."

To this the master answered, "You are also correct."

In any type of conflict resolution scenario, perspective plays a huge part in coming to an agreement. As you will discover, a question never has one answer because both the question and the answer is different for everyone, based on their perspective. The story of the arguing monks is likened to that of the Western analogy of seeing a glass as half empty or half full. Both are equal in water volume, but the difference is how the person views that glass. If you are arguing with your counterpart on whether the glass is half full or empty, then both of you will dig into your respective positions and an agreement will never be reached. Therefore, the key to persuading the person that you are right is first to acknowledge that they too are correct. Once the other side no longer is competing against you, then that's the turning point when both of you can start to work together.

Their Way versus Your Way

Up to this point, we have discussed how to reduce tension between both parties and how to create a favorable environment for negotiations to begin. Rapport has been established and they are ready to talk. There is still another barrier towards reaching an agreement. They want you to see their way and you want them to see your way. If you let this loose in the real world, negotiations will break down, tensions will flair again and you will be right back where you started. Don't try to persuade them to see your ideas. Don't exert pressure to get them to conform. Don't tell them that your way is better. Don't compete with them over positions. Instead do the opposite. The key to getting them to see your way and agreeing with your way is not to confront them on their ideas, or to reject them, but rather to acknowledge their ideas openly without resistance and then guide them towards solving the problem. Let the problem tell them what the best choices are and let them discover the truth for themselves.

There's No Magic behind Persuasion

Whenever people think of persuasion, the first thing that they associate it with is mind control. Persuasion is not mind control. Mind control is the five-dollar side show event at the local fair. Persuasion is nothing new because it is something that we see on a daily basis and we've become so used to it that we do not even notice it anymore. Whenever we turn on the television, pick up our mail, listen to the radio, pass billboards on the way to work—everywhere, we are bombarded with a creative assortment of persuasion techniques in the form of advertisements. Chances are that there are several pieces of persuasion sitting right in front of you right now. For some reason though, when people associate persuasion with face-to-face conversations, they think that it's mind control when really it is no different than a commercial advertisement. Persuasion is not about getting people to do what you want—it's about seeing things from their perspective and getting underneath those demands to find the real needs and interests that they have for themselves and then finding creative ways to meet those needs. That's all it is, plain and simple—find their needs, find a way to meet those needs, and you have persuasion.

Unlocking Them from Their Positions

When we are faced with a problem, our minds automatically come up with a solution to that problem that is reasonable and justified to us. This solution is known as our position. We commit ourselves to fulfilling that position. The problem is that this position is only one way—our way, of solving a particular problem. That problem might have a number of different solutions, but because we have committed ourselves to one position, we have inadvertently closed off our minds to other options that might reach the intended goal in a better way.

The key then in order to unlock ourselves from these positions it to focus on the underlying needs, concerns, fears, and desires that are the driving force behind our positions. These driving forces are known as our interests.

Often people assume that their interests are opposite of the other person. "If I want more, he wants less." "If I take a stance, then they will attack it." While this might be true for positional bargaining, it is not always true for interest-based negotiating. By looking past the positions, one can find that there in fact many compatible interests that they both share. For example, let say that a married husband and wife are on the verge of divorce. The husband is upset because he thinks that his wife is trying to control his life. The wife is upset because she feels that her husband no longer spends time or cares for her anymore. Where might their compatible interests lie?

- They both care for each other. It could very well be that neither one of them wants to take the divorce route and shouldn't have to either because underneath all the face-saving is the fact that both of them still have solid feelings for each other.

- They both want stability. Both parties enjoy the stability of being in a relationship. Neither one of them wants to contemplate the hardships or the stigma of being a divorcee.

- They both have investments in their children. This couple has equal stakes in their 4-year-old daughter.

- They both have stubborn personalities. The reason why these two got married in the first place is because they are very similar to each other. They both are stubborn and see things their own ways without trying to empathize with the other. The moment that one of them yells out the dreaded "D" word, means that the other has no choice but to call the bluff and sooner rather than later, both of them are signing divorce documents that never needed to happen in the first place.

So how can we use these interests to formulate a win-win situation for this couple? Positionally-speaking their focus of the dispute centered on the wife telling the husband that he had better stay in tonight or else. The husband does not like to be controlled and calls the bluff and leaves. So then the positional argument became centered on a threat of divorce, which was again called and now both are deadlocked because neither wants to appear like the weaker one and back down. By focusing their attention away from their position on divorce and directing it towards their needs, concerns, desires and fears, the couple can recognize that both still do love each other and that their interests are not opposed to each other—just differing. She desires more companionship and he desires more personal freedom. By recognizing that they share more compatible interests than opposing ones, it makes the task of creating a mutually-beneficial solution a lot less daunting.

Unlocking positions by using the physiological-emotional linkage. New studies have shown that our emotional states are directly tied into our physiological state as well and in a negotiation or mediation session, we can use this phenomenon to our advantage to break up a deadlock. If someone locks themselves into a position and are unwilling to budge, then instead of trying to pry that person out of their position, get them to stand up or move around. Studies have shown that when a person locks themselves into a position, their body becomes also locked into position. Try overcoming their deadlock by getting them to change their body position.

Ask Questions to Uncover Interests

So far we have learned how to reframe an opponent into a partner and how to reframe verbal attacks away from us and onto the problem. Now we must use reframing to focus on interests instead of positions. Remember that positions are the wants and the interests are the needs. We can use the power of nonconfrontational questioning to refocus your counterpart's attention onto their needs and allow them to discover their interests.

The real beauty of nonconfrontational questions is in the fact that they offer no target for attack, like statements do. Questions have the power to educate the person on what the problem is rather than causing conflict by telling them what the problem is.

- Uncover their interests from their positions
- State our own interests and concerns
- Work together to solve the problem

<u>Examples of open-ended questions:</u>

- "Who can help us with this project?"
- "Help me understand why this is important to you."
- "Where can we go to take care of this together?"
- "What are your main concerns here?"
- "How can I help to make this better for us?"
- "What can we do better so that we don't run into this problem in the future?"
- "When can we get together to talk about this issue?"
- "What makes you happy?"
- "How can I help make this better?"

Ask general questions. These questions are used to allow the other side to point the direction of the conversation. General questions are non-threatening and make them feel like you care about them as a person rather than just collecting information. General questions can be opinion-seeking questions or they can focus on how the person is feeling. Ask general questions about the person's needs, interests, and concerns.

- "What are your interests here?"

- "What do you consider the most important things?"
- "Help me understand why you want that."

Ask specific questions. After the other side has set the direction for the conversation, follow their answer up by digging deeper beneath their answer to uncover their hidden motivations. What are their main concerns specific within that issue? Whenever you ask a general question, you are going to get a general answer. It is very unlikely that people will automatically give you all the details to that question because they don't feel obligated to share everything initially with you. It becomes your job to whittle down each layer of their answers until you left with only the pure motivating factors underneath their positions.

- "Why do you feel it's important to lay off 25 workers?"
- "How come you want to divorce him?"
- "Why don't you want to take out the trash today?"

Paraphrase to confirm. Just like what we used during active listening, paraphrasing allows you to confirm the interests that your counterpart has told you. This reduces any chance of misinterpretation and it has the important effect of drawing the person's attention closer to the specific interests that you have touched on when asking specific questions. You might also find it necessary to ask more questions regarding their interests after paraphrasing. Keep asking questions until you distill the prime motivators behind their behavior.

- "So what I'm hearing is that your main concern is with the fiscal budget of the company. Is that right?"

Make sure you use nonconfrontational questioning. The difference between confrontational and nonconfrontational questions is that confrontational questions make the person react defensively about their actions.

- "I need this done by 5 PM."
- "Why?" (confrontational question)
- "Because I said so. Just do it."

See how asking with "why" caused the person to become defensive? Non-confrontational questions avoid the pitfalls of making the other person react defensively by approaching the same question indirectly.

- "I need this done by 5 PM."
- "Sure. That's pretty soon. Is there a particular reason it needs to be done so quickly?
- "Well, I'm leaving for a business trip tomorrow and I need this report for my presentation."

Avoid close-ended questions. Close-ended questions are those questions that can be answered "yes" or "no." Close-ended questions don't bring anything useful to the negotiation process because they require little, if any, thought process on their part to answer. "Did you have fun today?" "Yes." "Can I get a refund?" "No." These types of questions are not intuitive. They do not actively engage the problem-solving ability of the other side. Instead, make your questions open-ended. Give them a question for which they don't already have a scripted answer. The whole purpose of asking nonconfrontational questions is to get them to start thinking about the problem and ways of solving it.

Question and pause. Silence is a powerful tool in the reframing process. Psychologically, silence tends to make people uncomfortable and that discomfort is what persuades them to talk. Ask a question and then pause to give them time to think about the question. Don't let the silence compel you to break it by saying something. Instead, let them break the silence with their answer.

Detailed questioning. There are very few places that have not been invaded by the scam-artists of today. They have even invaded our personal homes through telemarketing, infomercials, and the Internet. The prevalence of scam-artists and people trying to make a quick buck by promising a cure-all product and instead selling you a lemon is getting to be really difficult today to distinguish. It is hard to tell the difference between scams and legitimate businesses that are beneficial to your personal or professional life. How do you tell the difference between the two?

The filter that separates the quality product from its cheap plastic imitator are detailed, fact-finding questions. Scams and purveyors of cheap crap boost the glitz and glory of their product, while at the same time obscuring the specifics of the product. The scam artist will promise the world, but will not tell you how their service or product will get you there—without of course giving them your credit card number first.

When dealing with the fast-talking sales specialist, you are in a negotiation between their product and your money. They are trying to convince you that their product or service will outweigh your interest in the money that you have, thus making the sell. They accomplish this through what is known as blitzkrieg selling. They reach you when you least expect it (i.e. while eating dinner) and they promise you the world, while being very vague about what it is you are actually purchasing. They bombard you with fast-talk and interpret your silence as agreement. How many times have you heard a telemarketer tell you "So it sounds to me like you are interested? Let me just sign you up here then." If you choose to deal with a salesperson, then take control of the conversation by interjecting in their script and posing questions to them. Typical telemarketers will be reading from a prepared script, whereas, true sales representatives will cater to your concerns and questions. By interjecting and asking specific questions on how their product or service can benefit your current life or business, you can get into the real details of whether or not you want to conduct business with that company.

The Proud Archer

Once upon a time, a young archery champion challenged a master, known to have skill with the bow, to an archery contest. The young archer pointed to a distant tree out beyond the village. The young archer drew his beautifully decorated bow and shot the target dead on.

"Very impressive," said the master. "My old eyes have trouble even seeing at such a great distance."

"I am not finished yet," said the boastful archer. He took another arrow out, strung it and let it loose from his bow. The second arrow split the first arrow in half. "Haha. Since I hear you are the greatest master with the bow, I want you to beat that."

The master picked up his simple wooden bow and beckoned to the young archer to follow him up a mountain. They reached a ravine where there was a perilous chasm underneath and only a rotting log as a bridge. The master walked calmed to the center of the log which began to shake and creek with the master's weight. He pointed at a very close tree at the other side of the ravine. The master strung an arrow onto his old bow and let the arrow loose, hitting the target. "Now it is your turn," said the master.

The young archer took one look at the bottomless abyss underneath him and was too frightened to step out onto the log. The master said to the archer, "My friend, you have much skill with the bow, but little skill with the mind that lets loose the shot."

A skilled negotiator knows not to play someone else's game for it is a game that cannot be won. Instead, they change the frame of the game to make it fair for both sides. In a negotiation, when one side makes demands and expects concessions, they will expect that you will play their game just as the young archer knew that the master could not make the long shot from his front door step. Rather than compete with your counterpart on their turf, change the nature of the game, just as the master illustrated to the young archer that there is more to archery than being skilled with the bow.

Persuasion Tactics

This section will deal with some useful tactics to aid you in your quest to reach an agreement with the other side. Keep in mind that persuasion used in the Street Negotiation context is not manipulative or deceitful in nature. The goal is not to trick them into believing our word, but rather to get them to see that we understand their perspective and that we can come up with new options that might meet their needs in a better way than their ideas.

Bite-sized pieces. In any conflict, it's easy to become overwhelmed at the overall dispute when taken in as a whole. The big picture causes fear. It makes people think, "There's no way we can reach an agreement on this." It's like looking at a long algebraic formula—it looks intimidating at first and our initial reaction, especially if you hate math, is to immediately reject it. But an amazing thing happens if you take that long formula and you reduce it down into manageable portions that even a child can do. No longer does the person see the formula as an impossible equation to be solved, but rather as a series of manageable calculations that he has the ability to solve. The same holds true with conflict—break them down into bite-sized, individual issues and start with the easiest one.

Emotional reasoning. This is one of the most powerful persuasion techniques around and therefore can be subject to abuse, but a Street Negotiator should know that most people make their decisions based upon emotions, not logical reasoning. People just use logical reasoning to justify the emotional decisions that they make. Earlier in this book, we discussed thinking with your rational mind instead of your emotional one. The flip side to this is that the emotional mind is quite susceptible to persuasion. Instead of laying out the logical reasons why someone should do something, you might want to describe how it makes you feel and the benefits that it will have to their own life. "It would make me so happy if you did this for me. And it would also bring us closer together too," instead of, "This is the right thing to do."

Persuasive power of conviction. Police officers are taught about using command presence when dealing with unruly people. Command presence is the air of authority—of saying and acting with enough confidence that people believe that you know what you are doing. People are heavily influenced by someone who has conviction in their words and this can be translated for use in a negotiation. When speaking, you do not want to talk as if you don't know what you are saying. Instead, speak with 100% conviction and make sure your body language mirrors that conviction. You will find that you can persuade a large majority of people just based on how convincing you sound.

Treat *"No"* as a reaction, not a word. We must condition our minds to accept that the word *no* is not a word, but rather an autonomic reaction that is independent of conscious thought. This is similar to the reaction a person experiences when they touch a hot kettle—they immediately jerk their hand back, saying "ouch." Why do we automatically do this when we touch something hot? It is because this reaction is programmed within us to whenever we experience something that can cause us danger or harm. Just like our reaction to heat, we also react in a similar way to social exchanges that cause fear or uncertainty. We say *no*, not because we necessarily mean *no*, but because we are experiencing uncertainty or fear. We say *no* because we are programmed to say *no*, but it is important to remember in a conflict situation that *no* does not equate to *never*. *No* is simply a starting point in reaching *yes*. Think of *no* the same way as when a person takes a defensive stance against you. Their mind is set to defend and sometimes even to attack you in order to keep you back. By pushing them into a corner or becoming defensive yourself, you only act to further their opposition against you, which is why adding pressure to someone who has reacted with a *no*, only makes them hold onto that reaction much more tenaciously.

The key to overcoming *no*, is to acknowledge their uncertainty, uncomfortableness, and fear. Just as an animal handler knows not to corner a frightened animal, so should you not corner a frightened counterpart by increasing pressure, becoming defensive, or moving in closer. Instead, back away from them and give them space to breathe. Show them that you pose no threat to them and give them an exit door to escape from other than directly through you.

Command & control if you're young. If you are young, then unfortunately you are going to be conflicted by yet another obstacle in the negotiation—your age. If the other side is much older than you, they will perceive your youth as inexperience, or incompetence. Therefore, as a young person, you have to take a no non-sense approach to negotiating and make sure that sniping does not occur. Let them know that you mean business and that your age has nothing to do with the objective.

Don't fall prey to the fact that they have time over you because often it is the most experienced ones who fall accustom to being complacent in a negotiation because they have been doing it for so long. View your youth as an advantage, not a weakness and take charge of the situation.

How to say *"No"* **without rejecting claims.** Telling your counterpart *no* without causing resentment or anger is a tough skill to learn, but there are two main ways to tackle this dilemma—you can use a delay tactic or you can reframe the statement internally. Police negotiators are trained not to say "no" to a hostage taker because it is both negative and confrontational in nature—two things that the hostage negotiator wants to avoid. To get around the unreasonable demands that the hostage taker might make, the negotiator will use a delay and distract tactic and tell the hostage taker something like, "I'll see what I can do about that…In the meanwhile, is there anything else I can do for you?" By doing this, the negotiator has not openly said no to the terrorist and he has immediately diverted the terrorist's attention away from this question with one of his own.

Another way of saying "no" without directly using that two-letter word is by telling the person reflecting the statement inward by saying, "I'm sorry. I just can't." Saying "no" is confrontational because it puts you against them and creates conflict. By telling the person that you can't do it, it reflects the same information inwards and does not make the situation confrontational.

Turn your opponent into your partner. Even though you have effectively reduced your counterpart's tension against you, their perspective might still be a win-lose battle just like the two captains. Their main strategy will be to defend their own position while attacking you personally. The first step towards unlocking them from their position is to change your own internal perspective about the person you are dealing with. Instead of being opponents against each other, picture yourself as partners, working on helping each other achieve a common goal. This does not mean you have to be friends with, or even like your partner, but you need to work with him rather than against him.

Acknowledge their ideas rather than reject them. Whenever someone states a position that we don't agree with, our first inclination is to reject it by saying, "No." This works against the negotiation however because it causes the other side to take offense to that and defend their ideas by digging into their position even more. Rejecting what your counterpart says turns the relationship into an "I" versus "You" confrontation which does not facilitate any type of cooperative behavior. By acknowledging their ideas as a possible solution, you effectively draw your counterpart closer to you rather than push him away. Acknowledging their ideas does not mean you have to agree with them, it simply means that you accept what they say as part of the discussion of the problem that you both face.

When someone makes a you statement that is directly attacking you, then the best way of dealing with that statement is acknowledging it and listening to their concerns. Realize that when someone is making you statements, they are angry or frustrated and they need their concerns to be heard and acknowledged with unconditional acceptance. They don't want a confrontation because that would only serve to stoke the fire of anger within them. The proper water to dose that fire is using your active listening ability to defuse them.

Attack the problem—not the person. Often when a mutual problem arises, people tend to mix up the problem along with their relationship and attack both as if it were one. This is the source of much conflict because the person is attacking the problem, but because he sees his counterpart and the problem as one, he inadvertently attacks his counterpart in the process. The key then is to separate the problem (substantive issues) from the relationship. You want to be kind and understanding to your partner, while at the same time attack the problem aggressively and mutually.

Bring out their desire to help. One of the best strategies for asking for compliance from someone is to ask for help or advice. This works because you are making them help you with the problem instead of competing against you and also it creates a bond between you that will be difficult to break later on. Most people want to help if and when they can and this is a powerful way to gain their compliance. Instead of telling them to do something and being confrontational with them, simply reframe that comment into one that asks for their help.

Try to find something that the person is passionate about and ask about that to get his mind off the position that he has dug into. When you are engaged in Street Negotiations, don't feel that you have to lock yourself into a role of power. Sometimes being the naïve or vulnerable one can be the most powerful negotiation tool you have.

Discuss compatible interests. With the other side focusing so much on their wants, they might not see that their interests are much more similar to your own interests than they thought. Highlight your compatible interests with them and use that as a springboard to discuss options later on.

Get them to invest in you. We often believe that in order to persuade somebody, we must show them our generosity. While they might appreciate our gifts or hospitality, persuasion only happens when they invest in you. This is because we have a psychological tendency to feel more attached to people into whom we have invested our time or attention. Also, by allowing them to give you gifts or hospitality, you are allowing them to feel good about doing good for themselves, thereby creating a powerful association between their feeling good and you.

Be like them. The misconception is that opposites attract, which is not necessarily true. Opposites make us curious and play to our adventurous nature, but we are more attracted to people who are like us because it makes us comfortable. This strategy can be used in persuasion by adjusting your nature to mirror that of your counterpart. Be more like them and you will have more leverage to influence them.

The persuasive power of deadlines. As a negotiator, you should learn to love deadlines. Most of the major exchanges in a negotiation are made within the last moments before the deadline is up. When another side suggests a deadline, be happy because a deadline means that they are working with you, not against you. How so? Well, a deadline means that both of you value your time, and therefore are agreeing to work together against the clock in order to save time. Think back to the time when you had to write a term paper, or had been given an assignment to complete. If you were given several months to complete the assignment, chances are that you would start working on that term paper towards the later end of that deadline. The same psychology goes with a negotiation. People don't want to make concessions or decisions too early and if they feel that they have all the time in the world to make a decision, then the negotiation could drag on. Remember from our earlier chapter that the person with the most time typically has the most power in a negotiation. Ask the other side to set a deadline for both of you, so that you can judge their value on time in the negotiation. Try not to be limited by the restraints of time and you will find that deadlines are you best friend.

Control your tendency to feel pressured when someone makes an unreasonable deadline and learn to recognize a deadline when you see one. In the crisis situation, a deadline is really easy to spot because it comes as a form of a threat—a jet and a bag of money in twelve hours or hostages start dying. In the civilian world, deadlines are less dramatic, but nonetheless they serve the same action—to make you decide under pressure. "Buy now—only one hour left." "If you want it today, I can take off an additional $200." There is a difference between real deadlines and fake ones. You can easily tell if the person's deadline is fake or not by simply probing into their level of power and their value on time. Who has the time constraints—you or them? If it's them, then they are not in the position to be setting unreasonable deadlines and it's best just to ignore them and focus on the real task of uncovering interests.

Deadlines are best when each side has an opportunity to establish rapport and communicate their needs with each other. Therefore, deadlines should be presented after the reduce tension step in the process to maximize efficiency. That way, rapport has already been established and setting a deadline furthers the cooperation process along towards agreement. Throwing out a deadline, especially at the onset of a negotiation, can cause resistance, especially if the other side views it as unreasonable.

Funny money. There is a psychology to spending that credit card companies and Vegas casinos know all too well. That is the psychology of funny money. A person with twenty dollars in cash is going to spend that twenty dollars as efficiently as possible by looking at brands, prices, and various options before making his selection. On the other hand, that same person might go to a casino and lose fifty dollars on one hand of blackjack. What's the reasoning with that? It has to do with our perception of money. We perceive cold hard cash to be real money and non-physical money to be something less than real money. How can you apply this as a tactic? In several ways. If you are a seller and you have traditionally only accepted cash as a means of conducting business, then you are missing out on the virtues of accepting funny money in the form of credit cards. If you are negotiating on the price of a larger item and you are both deadlocked on the price because it is too much for him to spend at once and you cannot go down any lower, then use the concept of funny money to your advantage. By simply offering it for a monthly payment, rather than a lump sum, you can successfully get more funny money than the overall price because you are enacting the funny money tactic on the other person. Remember that when you ask for cold hard cash—you are asking for real money, hence locking them to a set price. If you ask for funny money, you are unlocking their box to greater options.

Visual understanding. Most people have an easier time understanding something if they can see it in front of them. If you can manifest your words into something physical that can be seen or even better felt, then that would increase your chances at persuading the other person.

Ask "what if." Rarely is a price non-negotiable. When someone digs into their position and holds onto it adamantly, it might be difficult to get around it. One powerful tactic you can use to dig underneath their position is to ask "what if" questions. These questions make the person shed more information about the reasons why they have stated a price by probing hypothetical examples and getting them to answer them. "How much would it be if I bought 50…100." "What if I paid all cash right now?" The power of "what if" questions is that they focus on uncovering information regarding how the other party sets their prices and conducts business. "What if" questions work like a probe to uncover your partner's decision-making process.

The persuasive power of print. Believe it or not, there is some truth in the adage that, "If it's in print, then it's got to be true." Although the wide spread circulation of tabloids and web-pages that are floating around nowadays has diminished the effectiveness of all types of print, it still holds true that the printed word is one of the most persuasive physical tools that you can use in a negotiation. This is because it unconsciously changes your counterpart's frame of mind about who you are. It lends credibility to your name and it turns you from an average person, into a professional. It is therefore no wonder why corporations spend billions of dollars on graphic design and corporate identity marketing. People today are more knowledgeable about they type and source of printed material that's out there and not all will have the same affect. You might have a personal blog on a website somewhere, but that is not going to lend any credibility to your name. A printed and published article in a respected publication, an authored book, a professional website, or a published review can greatly enhance the way you are viewed by other people. Likewise, reviews and objectively published material about your company or product will have the same effect of establishing trust and credibility. In establishing a fair standard, having a printed copy from a well-respected source (i.e. legal source book, blue book, etc) instantly persuades the other person to accept that standard as being the truth. Printed material is one of the biggest persuasion techniques around, so you must use it with ethical restraint and not as a dirty tactic to mislead.

The rule of six. Overcoming resistance to a new idea, suggestion, or favor can be difficult at first. Most people ask once and give up after the first decline. Seasoned negotiators know that persistence is a powerful persuasion technique in and of itself because it breaks down that initial resistance. The general rule among negotiators is never assume that a deal is off until it's been asked at least six times.

Don't be a bureaucrat, be human instead. Especially in our professional lives, we have a tendency to lock ourselves into being too professional, which is fine for customer service, but bad for one-on-one conflict. Being an emotionally-apathetic bureaucrat is exactly the opposite of what you want to do when someone is angry or upset because they will see you as cold and uncaring. Instead, push aside the professional face and relate to the person from the stand point of one human to another. Tell them a self-depreciating story about your life, or open up to them on a personal level.

Use humor. Sometimes it is not enough to simply counter the tactic that they are using because they might just resort to another one to see what exactly they can get away with. It then becomes necessary to let them know that you know what tactic they are using. This usually gets them to stop, but the trick is doing it in a way that they won't perceive it as an attack. You can do this by mixing it in with humor. "Hahaha, that was the best tag team routine I've ever seen. Seriously, though—let's get back to the issue."

Counter Tactics for Unfair Tactics

To be a good Street Negotiator, you are going to have to know some of the common tricks of the trade. The following are some unfair persuasive tactics that many people choose to employ. They are unfair because they enact some very powerful psychological principles of human behavior and therefore throw off the balance of a principled negotiation. This is not a course on ethics, but a true Street Negotiator would adhere to the set principles and guidelines of interest-based negotiation and stay clear from using these deceptive pop-psychological tricks.

They check you, you check them. Every decent sales person is taught to get the client to commit themselves on paper while they are there in the office or room. They are taught that a potential buyer's willingness to make the purchase diminishes over time after the presentation is made. They are right. A person's emotional mind does all the buying and the rational mind just tries to justify it. Sometimes, the pressure to get the client to commit themselves on paper during the initial presentation is so great that it becomes a very unfair tactic. How do you counter such a tactic without getting frustrated and angry? Use the *reverse credit check technique*. When you go to a car dealership to purchase a new car, they don't just sell you a car based on your word that you have good credit. They do a thorough credit history check on you to make sure that you *can* pay. Well, if you are getting pressured by them to sign, do the equivalent of a *"credit check"* on them. By this I mean, ask to verify the information that they have provided you through an impartial third party or known industry standard for accuracy before you commit to the deal. No one can argue that such a thing is unfair. If they put up a fuss, then just use the example that a car salesman wouldn't accept just your word of good credit before handing you a car, so why should you accept everything that they say as the truth without doing some research of your own to authenticate their facts and figures.

False facts and figures. A commonly used dirty trick in negotiation is the use of facts, figures, and statistics. This is because numbers have a very powerful ability to persuade people, mainly because they seem scientific and objective and they confuse a good majority of people. Whenever another party throws complex facts, figures, statistics or studies at you without fully explaining them in English, then this should be a red flag that they are attempting to persuade you with numbers. Almost any statistic or fact, objective or not, can be taken out of context and presented in a misleading fashion. If the person is really dirty, then the facts and figures themselves might be false. To prevent yourself from being persuaded by facts and figures, ask for clarification on anything that you do not understand. Even if you do understand that information, play dumb and ask the person to explain them to you. If they are knowledgeable and fair, the honest counterpart will show you step by step how the numbers and facts were established and will not hesitate for you to verify this information. The second counter tactic is to have your own independent facts and figures to compare. This means do you homework and collect your own data. Then if the other side decides to use this tactic on you, you will have all the ammunition you need to call him on that tactic.

Fait accompli. Fait accompli is a negotiation tactic that basically means, what is done is done. While most people are not familiar with the term, it is a well-used tactic amongst diplomats and negotiators alike. In a Street Negotiation sense, the fait accompli is unknowingly implemented in our day to day lives. Say John wanted his business proposal implemented by his company so he takes it to the manager. His manager denies his proposal, saying that the company has already made a decision on the matter and nothing can be done now. The effect of this tactic is that it effectively ends a negotiation without much effort by your counterpart and really there is no counter to it either. So how do you deal with this tactic? You must bring the person back to the table by showing them that negotiating with you is better than the consequences of a non-agreement. In this example, John might convince his manager that his plan will save the company a huge amount of money.

"Take it or leave it" How many times have we heard this commonly used negotiation tactic? The "take it or leave it" tactic is basically an ultimatum designed to prevent further negotiations from happening. It is almost always a bluff and a challenge to the other side to see who has the stronger nerves. The problem with this tactic is that it causes too much resistance and conflict to facilitate an agreement. This tactic is aggressive and demanding, two things that don't sit well with your counterpart. What you are basically saying with this tactic is, "It's going to be my way, or no way." Now the other side is going to have to reassert their own dominance over the situation by choosing to "leave it" rather than to "take it" to save face and show you who really is in charge. Where is the negotiation now? There are three ways you can counter the "take it or leave it" tactic. The first way is by simply ignoring it. Let it fall on deaf ears and just continue negotiating like you never heard it. This lets you test the seriousness of their threat. The second way is by asking them, "What do you think might happen if we don't reach an agreement." This will get the other side to realize the consequences of not reaching a negotiated settlement. The third counter to this is to focus on the other side's needs and interests and move them away from their demands. Once you find compatible interests with them, then they will see you as a partner and not an adversary.

Highball / Lowball. When your counterpart makes the initial offer and it is far beyond reasonable by being either too high or too low, this is what is known as highballing (if it's high) or low-balling (if it's low). The other side throws out an unreasonable number knowing that they will concede small while trying to get you to concede bigger, making the middle ground more in their favor. You can counter highball prices by asking how they came up with that price and ask for an itemized breakdown of that estimate. You can and always should research the market price for that service or good and use competitive advantage to justify them lowering their unreasonable offer. As the consumer, you typically have the advantage because the seller wants your business; therefore, they are more committed to the deal than you are, giving you more power. If you are the seller and the client uses a low-ball tactic on you, then you can ignore the tactic and discuss what is important to them. You can also discuss what is the competitive rate or price for your service or product and describe the added non-monetary benefits of doing business with you.

False alliance. This is the tactic where the salesman attempts to build trust with you by bad-mouthing a particular brand of product in order to sell you the more expensive one. This tactic works because they show you a base model and make their pitch on it, and then they pull you in closer, as if they were sharing some secret advice with you and they tell you what's bad about the product or its defects. By doing this, they have established a certain trust alliance with you because now you believe that they have just told you this information and valued you over the sale. But their true intention is to use that established trust as a weapon against you to sell an even pricier model to you. Counter this tactic by telling the person that you only want to spend in a certain price range and that more expensive models are out of the question. If they are truly genuine about their alliance with you as a person, then they will use their expertise to help you find one that is within your budget, even if it means going to a competitor.

Flinching. Flinching is a psychological tactic where one side makes an offer and the other side acts surprised and insulted like it was totally unreasonable. This causes the first person to lower their overall expectations for the offer and make more concessions to the other side. A simple way to combat this tactic is to reaffirm the criteria that you used in coming to that particular offer or price.

Some people, particularly people who are new to making purchases in a particular industry may think that your prices are unreasonable because they don't know what the going rate or price is for that service or product. It then becomes your job to educate them with a series of objectively fair standards to show them that your rates are quite reasonable.

The mark-down. There is a psychological rule that people follow when making a decision. That rule is called comparing and contrasting and the infomercial industry has exploited this tactic to its limit. When we make a decision, we compare it and contrast it with other like values. In the case of an infomercial, they present a higher price than you would expect to pay, say $200 for a blender. Then they slash the price and offer it to you at $125. They are placing their bets that you will compare and contrast the price differences and feel that you are getting a really good bargain. Whenever you are faced with a mark-down, first ask the question "Are they marking their price down from the fair market value or their own contrived mark-up?" To answer this question you will need to know the fair market value of the product or service so that you can judge from where they are marking that price down.

Good guy / Bad guy. There are many varieties of this old school tactic that still suckers people every time. The most commonly used variant of this is the imaginable bad guy, usually in the form of the unseen boss, manager, or supervisor who the salesman has to talk with in private before getting approval for the deal. Of course, the salesman is the good, righteous, and fair one, and the invisible tyrannical boss is the bad guy. The salesman wants to make you see them as more friendly and personable than their boss to gain your compliance for the deal. There are two basic ways of countering this persuasive tactic. The first is that you can recognize their tactic and call them on it using humor. "Hahaha. That was the best good guy/bad guy routine ever. Thanks for the laugh. Now seriously, let's do some business." Just remember not to patronize them or attack them for using this tactic or you will create resistance. The second, and more suggested, method of dealing with the good guy/guy routine is to simply do the same thing back to them. First recognize the tactic and then counter it by using your own tyrannical money manager, usually in the form of a spouse or loved one who is not there with you. "You know, I'd love to sign with you, but I'll have to run this by the wife (husband) first. I'm not sure they will like this new estimate." By doing this, you will effectively be using the same tactic that police hostage negotiators use. They don't have any power to grant requests. They merely listen and exchange requests. It is the crisis team commander who makes the decisions on what is a reasonable request to grant. By taking the decision-making power out of your hands and making your spouse the commander, you will have effectively leveled the playing field.

The bandwagon. People tend to think in a way that is consistent with everyone else. If everyone thinks Bob is a nice person, then chances are that you will think he is a nice person too. This bandwagon effect can be used as a tactic against you if you are not careful. A salesman might try telling you that three people before you have just bought that type of car and that they are selling "like hotcakes." That salesman is using the bandwagon tactic on you because they know that if you believe other people are getting that car, you will desire it more too. You need to be able to judge the quality and nature of something through your own filter and not through the behaviors of other people.

No authority to grant requests. This is a common tactic in large corporations. You will be trying to negotiate with someone who has no authority to grant any of your negotiated requests in the first place. This works for them because they will attempt to persuade you with nothing to lose or concede because they can always default to the saying, "I'm sorry, but this decision will have to be made by the president of the company." The way you counter this tactic is to make sure that you are dealing with the right person in the very beginning. Don't automatically go straight to the top either as this can be another source of resistance (see how to deal with a bureaucrat). Find the person who is willing to talk with you and make sure that they have the ability to help you out.

Big favor & mini favor. This tactic is common among manipulators. Initially they ask for an outrageous favor from you, half-knowing that you will decline their request. They then immediately follow up their big favor with a smaller favor, exploiting the psychological rules of compare and contrast decision-making to make their smaller (and usually intended favor) more realistic to you. They are hoping that in contrast to the larger favor, the smaller one will be no big deal to you. Counter this tactic by simply declining again. If you believe that your second decline of their offer will be met with resistance, then a good tactic is to use their own tactic against them. Decline their second favor and immediately follow it up with a ridicules impossible favor of your own. Make sure that it is something that they could never do. They will decline you and you both will be back to a balanced karmic state.

Add-ons. It seems like where ever you go now to purchase electronic goods nowadays, you always get asked if you want insurance with that—in a not-to-dissimilar way that a fast food clerk asks if you want to super-size that meal. This is because some marketing genius somewhere discovered the potential for back-end sales using the add-on technique. No one I have ever spoken to who has purchased a retail insurance plan has ever made use of it. It's a worthless purchase that costs a lot. The counter for this is to ask them why you would need it. Is there something wrong with the products that they sell that they would need additional insurance with it?

Job title does not make them an expert. We often make the general mistake of assuming that just because someone works at a particular job or is dressed a certain way, that they are automatically an expert on the subject. While it might be true that they know a thing or two about the topic that they work in, it would be wrong to ask them expert advice without first scrutinizing their credentials. Case and point. A college student working at a computer store may know a thing or two about computers, but they might just be working there because it was the first or only job that they could find during their summer break. To assume that they know everything about computers or that they have the experience, training, and knowledge to be able to give you advice on what you need would be fool hardy. A properly trained salesperson would obviously suggest to you the highest end model. Spend time picking at the person's brain and seeing just how knowledgeable they are in the subject matter being discussed before you commit to their advice.

Getting it in your hands. This tactic is the classic for the car salesman. He knows that if you are able to drive around in the car, then you will become more attached to it and hence more willing to purchase it. Instead, spot this tactic early on and do not commit yourself to going for a test drive, or getting too attached with the purchase. This involves knowing your level of self-control and having a plan ahead of time as to whether or not you will test the product out.

Quoting rules, policies, and laws. There might be times when you are faced with dealing with a person who uses rules, policies, or laws to dictate what their negotiating behavior is and tell you that there is nothing they can do because it is right there in the manual. The counter for this tactic is to ask them the purpose of that rule and the intent behind that rule and whether that intent applies to your unique situation or not. Rules are a set standard way of handling things, but as we know, the world is not a standard place, so you have to convince the person to look at your present situation as a unique case. Many people don't realize that they can cross out, rewrite, or revise a contract. In fact, many people who write contracts don't know that the other side can change it. This is because we are so used to skimming over the words without understanding them and then haphazardly putting our signature on the dotted line. Rules, policies, and even laws are written by people and people are not always right. Think about it. Not too long ago, there were legalized racial segregation laws enacted by government entities. The bigger picture needs to be addressed when someone is quoting regulations. What is the intent behind those rules and does that seem righteous?

Setting Ground Rules

When things get really tough in a negotiation, it may become necessary to focus in on how the negotiation process is being conducted in order to change the process from an adversarial one to a cooperative one. Negotiate on the rules of negotiation. Sometimes, the place to start is by first agreeing to establish some ground rules for negotiating. Usually when things begin to break down, it is because no ground rules have been established and it takes the more responsible party to take a step back and address the point that arguing is getting neither party closer to agreement and that in order to prevent future arguing, some simple ground rules should be established. So what ground rules? Things like:

- We each take turns talking without interruption.
- No profanity.
- No blaming.
- No disrespect.
- No accusations.

The choice of grounds rules are up to you, but remember that both you and your counterpart must agree on these rules.

Step V

P
E
R
P

Options

S

We can try to avoid making choices by doing nothing, but even that is a decision.

~ Gary Collins

Now that everyone's interests are out on the table, it is time to brainstorm options and ideas for a solution. This is where the real cooperative side of Street Negotiation takes place because it deals with both parties working together, rather than fighting each other with concession giving or taking. During this process, you will be exchanging various ideas and options for a possible solution. Some of these ideas you might like—some of them you will disagree with. The same goes for your ideas. The key when brainstorming options is to acknowledge your counterpart's ideas as one possible solution, even if you disagree with it and conversely, you want to welcome criticism of your own ideas because they might see a flaw in it that you did not catch. By communicating with each other and showing respect for each other's ideas, you can facilitate some mutually beneficial options.

How to Invent Options

- **Identify the problem.** It sounds like common sense that you should know what the problem is before creating options that might remedy that problem. However, your interpretation of the problem might be different than what your counterpart sees as the problem. Therefore you want to make sure that both the other side and you have the same definition of what the problem is before moving on.

- **Identify causes.** Now that you know the problem, think of the possible causes of that problem. Or you can define the problem by comparing it to another similar situation with no problem and trying to find out what is different between the two.

- **Suggest possible remedies.** In this step, you need to find out what can be done to remedy the problem both of you are facing. What have others done in the past to remedy similar situations? You will want to examine both short term and long term remedies.

- **Create an action plan.** In this step, you expand upon the options that are most promising for your particular situation. This means that you examine these possible remedies in full detail and create a step-by-step action plan for carrying it out. This will enable you to fully discriminate between the options and decide which one you want to carry out. The added benefit of creating a step-by-step guide for implementing the option is that it makes the whole scope of the process less intimidating for the other side. Bite-sized pieces are much easier to swallow than the entire steak, so by cutting up the option into manageable pieces, you will gain their compliance much easier.

#1 Important Step for Creating Options

The barrier to creating and identifying options is that both sides criticize each other's contributions as being unreasonable or just plain wrong. Usually they favor their own options and so the whole process of creating options ends up as a positional negotiation in and of itself. How do you get the other side to hear your options? How do you unlock yourself from your own options so that you can get a broad idea of the entire range of options? The key is not to judge, evaluative, scrutinize, criticize, or weigh any of the options. Instead, merely list all the options that are possible in the current situation. Put them on a list or on the board in visible form for both parties to see. After all possible options are listed, then it becomes easier to identify those options that have the most benefit for all parties involved in the negotiation.

Brainstorming Cooperatively

Involve them in the process. One of the biggest areas of conflict when discussing options is for them to reject your options outright because they feel that those options are yours and not theirs. Instead of giving them a list of options to choose from, let them help you in discovering possible options that could work. Hold back on providing your own list of options until you have brainstormed ideas with your counterpart first. By involving them in the process of inventing options, you will gain their compliance in accepting the options that are generated.

Openly welcome criticism. It's our nature to defend our ideas when someone criticizes them. This causes conflict to occur. Instead, invite criticism and feedback of your ideas. Ask them if they see any problems with your ideas, or how they can improve it. Think of your ideas as a research paper you have written and you are giving it to your counterpart to edit and provide their fresh perspective on it.

Ask for advice. A Street Negotiator does not have all answers. No one does. Nor should anyone expect that a negotiator has all the answers.

Therefore, there is nothing wrong with asking your counterpart for advice. Perhaps they have training, experience, or education in a particular area that you do not. By asking them for advice, you are acknowledging their expertise in a particular area and it is also a form of flattery. They will be able to provide you with a fresh perspective on the situation for their angle and it will enhance the relationship by making them empathize with your own position.

- "What would you do if you were in my position?"
- "What would you suggest I do?"
- "You are much more experienced in this area than I am—do you have any advice that I can use?"

Build on their ideas. When the other side suggests an idea, work with it by building on that idea, adding or subtracting pieces of it, and molding it until that idea becomes the best option it can be. Just because you might not agree with an idea at first, does not mean that the idea can't be improved upon. Now is the time to start exploring those ideas.

Techniques on Dividing Property

You pick first, but I go twice. This technique is good if there is a lot of property to be divided. The concept is that the property is placed before both parties, either in a pile or on a list. One party will get to choose what they want first and the other side will get to choose two items after the first person is done. Then it alternates, with one party choosing once and the other party choosing twice.

I'll divide and you choose. This technique comes from the ageless story of two children fighting over a single orange and the mother who tells the first child that he can split the orange any way that he wants, but that the other boy gets to choose which portion he wants. Simple is it not? Yet when it comes to property, people lose sight of the simplicity of the technique and become engulfed in the power struggle, thinking only of concessions. If this happens to you, then remember the story of the orange and go back to simple principles that work—I'll divide the property into two piles that I believe to be equal and you choose which pile you want.

We'll create two equal piles, then I'll divide and you choose. Often is the case where there is only one item that is sought after by both parties. This might be a house, an office, or a car. What do you do when something cannot be divided equally and both you and your counterpart desire the property? The principle is the same as the first, except that another pile must be created. This is done by each party pitching into a second pile everything that they are willing to give up in order to obtain that property. The piles are evened up by agreement from both parties, then one person splits the piles equally and the other party chooses the pile that he wants.

Expanding the Pie

What happens when someone asks for an unreasonable price and you cannot use the power of competition in your favor? Too often we lock ourselves into a battle over price, but that is a futile effort. It's like two boys who are each given one half of an orange and told to negotiate with the other boy for a larger portion of the orange. It's just becomes a power struggle of egos or of positional strength when you try to negotiate over price alone. In the case of the orange, the boy who is bigger or stronger can force the weaker boy into giving up his half of the orange. Is this really what you want to do? Forcing somebody to do what you want because you are bigger, stronger, or have more power may get you what you want, but it leaves a whole lot of resentment, hurt feelings, and anger afterwards which will prevent a long-lasting relationship in the future. Also realize that there will always be someone who is bigger and more powerful than you are, so the key is not to resort to your power, but instead, broaden the options for trade.

Don't buy the entire orange, buy slices. Instead of arguing over a set price for a product or service, ask for a breakdown of those costs. Not only will it help you see where exactly the costs are going, but it will also make the other side analyze his price quote and force them out of the highball/lowball game. With the costs of the individual services broken down for you, you have an easier time negotiating the individual components of that service to make it fit within your budget. What features or services must you have and what can you live without? Often sellers will package a wide range of services or options to make the offer look more attractive, but really, who uses all those features? Try to pay for only the things that you will use to make it fit within your budget.

Don't trade apples for apples, maybe they want oranges instead. Cash is king—no one would argue that, but that does not mean that it is always the most valuable trade option in a negotiation. Say you wanted to rent some office space, but your counterpart asks for more money than you are willing to pay. Is this the final say? No—this is where your question-asking comes into play to uncover their needs and interests. Perhaps your counterpart is a business-owner and needs marketing materials. You are a graphic designer with marketing experience. It would be far more cost-effective for your counterpart to use you to produce his marketing materials rather than to spend his own time to track down a reliable designer. With you in his office, he can work directly with you on his marketing projects instead of doing some long-distance communication with some other designer. Your value to him exceeds that of the money he is asking for the office and that allows for a good trade to exist. Obviously, not all things work out this perfectly in the real world, but you never know what type of things can be traded in you don't probe the other side's interests and needs. Always be on the look-out for those low-cost/high-gain trades that you can make.

Identify their needs first. Before you even start to negotiate on the issue, be clear as to what the needs of your counterpart are because it could very well be that you are both negotiating over something that can be split in such a way as to satisfy both of your needs. Take the example again of the boys fighting over the orange. The most logical solution would be to split it in half, right? True, but perhaps one boy wants the fruit of the orange for eating and the other boy wants only the peel for baking. By first identifying the needs of both parties, it will give you more information as how to satisfy those needs in the most efficient way possible.

Focus on shared interests. One of the way in which you can invent options is by focusing on shared and compatible interests. These are not immediately visible during a negotiation because they often become hidden underneath the competing goals of each party. This is where questioning skills come into play to discover these interests. Once these shared interests are discovered, stress them as the basis for reaching an agreement. If two enemy sailors were stranded on the same island, they would most likely set aside their differences and focus in on their shared interest on working together to find a way back home.

Offer to help. Unless you're totally incompetent, inexperienced, or un-certified in a particular service, a way to expand the pie is to offer to help do the work that you can do yourself and pay for the things that you can't. Let the other side know what exactly you are capable and willing to do yourself and what you need them to do for you. Often when the price is too high, you can negotiate your own services into the deal to expand the pie and reduce cost.

Agree that you both disagree. Sometimes in a negotiation it would seem as if there was nothing compatible with the other side. However, differences can be the basis for an agreement also. You can both agree that you both disagree and this is a solid basis for several options. You can both agree to have the situation resolved by a third party or cast it out for a vote or agree to decide by looking up objective standards as a basis for decisions.

Shift perspectives. Sometimes the best way to invent options is to look at the problem from a variety of perspectives. How does your counterpart see the problem? How about an independent party? Or an expert? Change your perspective on the situation by stepping into the shoes of other people and you will effectively unlock your mind to a greater number of possibilities.

The dollar value of an apology. A simple, but genuine apology can sometimes be worth much more than money. People have waged tens or even hundreds of thousands of dollars on costly litigation in order to win a simple "I'm sorry" from the other party. Learn to see outside the "cash box" and learn what exactly is important to the other side as well as yourself.

Who Makes The First Offer?

Who makes the first offer in a negotiation? The answers to this question are as split as a political campaign. Some camps of negotiation say never to make the first offer because then you can't negotiate upwards and the other side will make a low-ball offer in an attempt to meet you somewhere in the middle. Other camps believe that the key to controlling the negotiation is to make the first offer so that you can control the starting point for negotiations. The Street Negotiator would decidedly not make the first offer until they have properly researched the issue at hand and discussed all the relevant details, needs, and interests with the other side first. After being armed with all the details about the purchase, the Street Negotiator has no problem in suggesting a first offer because they can back it up with objective criteria. This first offer does not have to be set in stone because there might be other non-monetary gains to be had in the negotiation, but it sets a fair point at which to negotiate from and it saves the hassle of playing the highball / lowball game.

Carrying and Leaving

Once upon a time, there were two monks who were traveling across the country together. One afternoon, they came to a river bank and saw a beautiful girl who was unable to cross the river. Seeing her difficulty, the elder monk volunteered to carry her across the river while the younger monk looked on in shock, for it was forbidden for monks to communicate with females. The beautiful girl thanked the elder monk for being a gentleman and both monks continued on until sundown and they found an old shack to sleep for the night. The elder monk quickly fell asleep while the younger monk twisted around, unable to calm his mind. Finally, the younger monk woke up the elder monk and scolded him for breaking their sacred rule.

"As monks, you know that we are supposed to stay away from women. You should be ashamed of what you did today!"

The elder monk looked at his troubled companion and told him, "Oh, so that is what has been bothering you. Brother, I have left the girl by the river, why are you still carrying her?"

Using Fair Standards

When you are discussing options with your counterpart, their option might be very different from your option. They contend that their option is fairer than yours and you argue the opposite. Who is right? How can options be discussed if both of you have differing views on what is fair. This is where fair standards come into play. Fair standards, or objective criteria, are the previous options that other people have used in similar situations as your own. If a merchant and a buyer are haggling over a necklace, then the typical positional-type bargaining will start with the buyer offering his lowest price, and the merchant offering it at his highest price i.e. low-balling/highballing. Well, not only is this inefficient, but it makes the process very arbitrary. Using a fair standard in this situation means that if you are the buyer and you go to that merchant, you offer him the going rate for that necklace based on the other merchants who are selling the same thing. Fair standards keep either side from playing the high/low game and it establishes a reasonable price right off the bat.

In mediation situation, where a third party is present, then the third party can act as the objective fair standard, granted that the mediator does not have any affiliation with either side. In a Street Negotiation, rarely will you ever have a third party present to lend an objective opinion, therefore the second best thing to a third party mediator is having a fair standard.

Steps to Using Fair Standards

1. **Agree that fair standards are appropriate.** In situations where money, property, land, or settlements are concerned fair standards should always be used to prevent either side from playing high/low. To save the time and hassle of haggling a deal based on arbitrary desires, agree to use a fair standard right away. This will ensure a principled negotiation.

2. **Ask them for the theory behind their options.** When your counterpart suggests a possible option, acknowledge it and ask them what makes it fair. This allows them to explain to you their basic principles that govern their views on fairness in their mind. It will also allow you to better understand their thought process for coming up with options.

3. **Make it objective.** Make sure that the fair standard is independent from either you or your counterpart. It should be something that is widely recognized as being a fair standard. For example, when you are buying a used car, a fair standard that many people use is the "blue book" value for that car.

4. **Adjust the fair standard to meet your situation.** While a fair standard might exist on a situation similar to yours, it might not be exactly similar to yours and will need to be adjusted accordingly. For example, if you are in the market for a used car and the salesman offers a competitor's ad for $10,000 as a fair standard, then you have to weigh into account factors such as the year, the mileage, add-on, damage, replacements etc. After factoring in all these other details into the figure, you might discover that the actual fair standard is $7500. You must negotiate with your counterpart on adjusting the fair standard to meet your particular situation as best as possible. Don't be stooped by falling for something just because it is in print.

5. **Agree on a fair standard.** It does not matter who suggests the fair standard or what details are adjusted in that fair standard; what matters is that both of you agree on using it to meet the purposes of your own negotiation. Once you agree to use a fair standard, you are already gaining some win/win outcomes that push you closer to a mutually successful negotiation.

Types of Fair Standards

- Industry standards.
- Well-known resources or publications.
- Agreed-upon experts.
- Appraisals.
- Fair market value.
- Competition.
- Policies, rules, laws.

Mediation as a Solution to a Deadlock

In the beginning chapters, we discussed the differences between negotiation and mediation. Remember that negotiation is a discussion between involved parties, whereas, mediation involves a neutral third party facilitator to help the disputing parties reach an agreement. Mediation provides the quickest route towards agreement because the mediator, being a neutral entity, serves as the fair standard for filtering options. This is why when negotiations come to a halt over the issue of what is a fair standard, sometimes it is easier to hire the services of a mediator to lend an objective view on this issue and suggest standards, which are proven to be neutrally fair to both sides. The advantages of having a mediator on hand lies not only with his ability to serves as a fair standard, but also by digging out the interests of both parties and then analyzing where the similarities lie. A mediator has the ability to collect all the proposals, needs, interests, concerns, and fears of both parties and then recommend a plan that is in the best interests of both parties and then have each party criticize the plan and reshape it until it is a product that both parties can agree upon. By doing this, the mediator has effectively used a win-win strategy of cooperation and now its both parties working on the problem rather than on each other.

Step VI

P
E
R
P
O

Solutions

Honest disagreement is often a good sign of progress

-Mahatma Gandhi

Reaching an Agreement

Inexperienced and sometimes even experienced negotiators relax during the closing part of the deal because they believe that the hardest part is behind them. This type of complacency usually leads them down the same path as the rabbit in the story. Don't think for a second that just because the other side has been agreeing with you up till this point that they will continue to agree with you when it comes time to close the deal because that's usually the time when they choose to pull the carpet out from beneath your feet.

Hostage negotiators know that the very end of a negotiation is also one of the most dangerous. This is because the process of surrendering involves trust and a whole lot of risk for both sides. The hostage taker is nervous because he is stepping out from behind his fortified position and his main concern is whether or not he is going to receive a bullet from the tactical team standing close by, or a sniper somewhere out on a rooftop. His trust in the negotiator's word is all he is holding onto. Consequently, it is also a trying time for the negotiator as well. He is relying on his trust of the hostage taker to follow a very strict procedure for surrendering so that no one gets hurt in the process. He has to make sure that both the hostage taker and himself are on the same page and that there is no miscommunication between them because one slight error could be disastrous. Say for example it was assumed, not directly communicated that the hostage taker not bring his weapon out when surrendering. The hostage taker is ready to give himself up, but has his gun in his hands when he steps out. This prompts the tactical team to issue threats for him to drop the gun, while aiming their MP-5's on him. This surprises the hostage taker who now believes that the negotiator lied to him and that the tactical team is there to kill him. The end result of this miscommunication is a gun battle, which will leave at least one person dead. From this example you can see how important it is to have good communication between parties so that there are no end surprises in store for either side during the closing process.

Barriers to Gaining Commitment

The reason why gaining commitment is so difficult is because of face-saving and the opposing support for your counterpart. Your counterpart has friends, family, and coworkers who are supporting his position and this makes it difficult for him to change that initial position if he feels that he will lose face in front of his supporters.

Face-saving is tied into integrity with one's own past thoughts and ideas.

People have a psychological tendency to act consistently with their prior ideas and deeds; therefore, this can become a barrier towards gaining a commitment if the other sees the commitment as conflicting with their prior ideas. The package offered to the other side might be a great deal to them, but if they feel that they are backing down or letting go of their prior ideas, then they will most certainly reject such an offer outright based on their own face-saving and integrity. It is therefore necessary to reframe the offer in a way that is continuous with their ideas and beliefs in order to allow them to save face.

Yet another barrier to gaining their commitment is the tendency for negotiators to start pushing their counterpart towards the commitment rather than having them reach it for themselves. People have a tendency to cut corners when the end is near because they get excited, but this pressure works counter-intuitively towards facilitating an agreement. Remember about perspective when coming towards an agreement. The end might be perfectly clear to you, but for the other side, it might not be as clear or they might need time to digest all the facts that have been presented to them. Pressure equals resistance and by pushing the other side towards the finish line, they are reactively going to push back away from it.

Don't Push, Guide Them

Imagine a rugged cowboy out on the American frontier guiding a bunch of steer across the plains and back to the ranch. How does he do it? The cowboy does not dismount off his horse, walk up to the steer and start pushing it in the direction of the ranch. That would be impossible. No, instead the cowboy shows the cattle a path and guides them in the direction that he wants. This is the mental image that you want to adopt when you are negotiating towards a commitment. Don't push them, rather guide them in the direction that you want.

Don't Feed Them Your Ideas, Let Them Feel Like You Both Created It

There is a tendency among us to tell people what we think they should do and to offer our own advice, but this often comes with some resistance because people don't like to adopt other people's ideas over their own. We desire a sense of free choice and therefore are more ready to accept ideas that are created at the table rather then being fed your prepackaged ideas. If you come up with a solution and present it to the other side, then they will view it as exactly that—your solution and not theirs and it will be viewed with some resistance. The key therefore is to refuse your desire to tell them a solution and rather guide them towards that solution, so that they feel it was invented together. You want to involve them in the process of reaching a solution and by doing so, you get the payoff of having them develop a greater sense of commitment towards the final agreement.

Offer Possible Solutions and Let Them Criticize Them

So far we have discussed guiding the other side towards your destination, but what happens when you encounter resistance? What happens when you ask them to help invent possible solutions and they can't or won't think of any? In order to breakthrough this barrier, you must offer them solutions and then ask them to criticize and revise that suggestion. It would appear that this goes against the prior suggestion of letting them create the idea at the table, but this is actually doing the same thing from their perspective. When an impasse occurs during a negotiation and the other side can't come up with the suggestion that you want them to invent on their own, then the alternative plan is to offer a suggestion to them and ask them to criticize it. "Well, how about this XYZ plan. Do you think it can work? Can you improve this idea?" By asking them to criticize and revise your suggestion, it has the psychological value of turning it from your suggestion into their own solution. It puts them in control because you offered the initial plan, but they made it into a final draft to their own liking.

Get it in Writing

Transferring an agreement from the mind into the physical world by placing it on paper is not only a furtherance of the agreement, but a symbol of that commitment that both parties share. Putting an agreement on paper enacts some very interesting psychological effects. The first is that any idea on paper is more readily identifiable and realistic than the same idea that remains in your head. Second, having that agreement on paper compels people to abide by that strategic flow of ink.

The interesting thing is that the word "contract" immediately conjurors up resistance in people. This is because not many people fully understand what a contract is because of all the legal jargon used in it and also because they associate contracts with greedy lawyers, conmen, and scummy landlords out to get them and their money. A contract is an agreement that is memorialized on paper and serves as the basis for establishing the rules and procedures mutual for the future. A contract sets guidelines and possible consequences for noncompliance. The contract is a powerful tool because it solidifies the agreement and compels the other side to fulfill their commitment to that agreement in the future. Taking someone up on their word is a good-hearted intention, but there are too many things that can go wrong with this. The person can forget. The person's interpretation of the agreement might differ from your own. The person might lie and state that they never agreed upon such things, knowing that you have no way to prove it.

Instead, take your time and find a sheet of paper and a pen and write up a simple agreement. It doesn't need to be neat—only legible. Call it for what it really is—a memorandum of understanding and treat it as a symbol of goodwill. There will be some people who will put up resistance to getting the agreement down on paper and their resistance is good because it should be a red flag to you that they have no intention of keeping their agreement with you. People know that if they have their agreement on paper, they are obligated to fulfill those commitments and this is a powerful psychological tool to get people to follow through on their commitments. You might even want to get in the habit of keeping a small notepad in your pocket to write agreements out for people in your daily interactions. People might think you're a bit *off*, but watch the percentage of people who make good on their commitments to you. I guarantee that it will go up.

Turning Options into Solutions

Don't rush. Many people get excited when generating options, anticipating that a closing deal is around the next corner; however, such a mindset will usually make the floor disappear beneath your feet. Such a case is when you are ready to close, thinking that all objections have been clarified or addressed and when going over the final solution, your counterpart objects to one or more items. Some people give up and let their emotional minds take over in a fit of frustration and that ruins the entire deal. You must stay calm and collected throughout this step, just like all the other steps.

Make it easy for them to say "yes." If your counterpart is almost at the point of closing, but still is unsure, then why don't you make it easier for them to give in by doing some of the work for them? Doing some of the work involved in closing a deal is a small concession to make, but it might mean all the difference to your partner. They might not have the time to write a contract, or make trips to the courthouse, so ease those worries by giving them these "freebies." It's an extra little nudge to get them to close with you.

Don't pressure them. Pressure increases stress and stress breeds conflict in a negotiation. By pressuring someone into a deal, you effectively have pushed them against the wall and they have no way out but through you. Give them time to think about a solution. If you are offering Nancy a watch for her husband and she's thinking about purchasing it for $800 and you tell her, "I'll give you five minutes to decide—take it or leave it." Then you have backed her against a wall with no options left for her. Don't corner anyone into closing a deal with the use of pressure. It breeds hostility and conflict in a negotiation.

Cold Feet

In many emotional or high-stakes negotiations some people might get cold feet at the end of the negotiation process just because it marks the closure of something. Many individuals get cold feet right before they sign marital settlement agreements for a divorce because it marks the official end of their relationship. It's scary for them because it is the beginning of a new way of life and its uncharted terroritory. If you are the other party and your counterpart gets cold feet right before the signing, don't explode out of frustration. This is the last thing you want to do because it will set the whole agreement backwards, and it will reaffirm to the other person that the agreement was not good in the first place. Instead, talk to them about their concerns and reaffirm the benefits of the agreement and reaffirm your relationship to that party. Some active listening is usually all it takes to push past the problem of cold feet.

Building a Dispute Resolution Plan into The Agreement

A good insurance policy to any agreement or contract that you make is to have an additional agreement on how future disputes will be settled. In many lawyer-written contracts, binding arbitration or lawsuits are the common clause in these contracts because that is what they are used to doing. However, be aware that arbitration or lawsuits will only serve to break-down the relationship of you and your counterpart because both have win-lose outcomes. Consider the benefits of first resolving conflicts with the aid of a neutral mediator who can facilitate a cooperative problem-solving plan with both of you before you have to go through costly and often needless litigation.

No Agreement? Use Your Plan B

Every negotiator will encounter a situation where the other side does not want to agree. What happens then? Is the negotiation a failure? The answer is no, the negotiating is not a failure because initially you sought to see if something better than what you could get on your own could happen through discussion. Well, if discussions did not turn up anything that would benefit you, then you still have your plan B to fall back on. How you implement your plan B is important however so lets take a look at what needs to be done.

Before You Walk Away From The Table

Ask them what the consequences will be. Before you implement your plan B, ask them what they think will happen if both of you walk away from the negotiating table. This reality-based questioning will make them focus on the true consequences of not reaching an agreement. The goal here is to make it hard for them to say "no" to you and you do that by offering them something better than their own plan B. If they are still focused on a win/lose outcome, then asking them what the consequences of not reaching an agreement will be makes them think hard about their own plan B.

Ask them what their plan B is. It's possible that your counterpart is overconfident about his plan B because he hasn't thought it through entirely. Question him about the specifics of it and highlight any flaws or negative aspects of his plan that you can see.

Don't threaten them. Using your plan B to threaten the other side is an aggressive tactic that will only lead to a bitter fight. A lot of divorces happen this way. A small argument happens and one person threatens a divorce, as more of a bluff than anything, but the other person has to save-face by calling that bluff and sooner than later, both parties are in the courthouse signing divorce papers that neither one of them wanted to sign in the first place. A threat turns a simple negotiation into a competition of power that result in both parties making unwise decisions for the sole purpose of hurting the other side. A lot of frivolous lawsuits happen this way. One side threatens to sue, the other side calls their bluff, and the other side has no choice but to save face and file the paperwork, and the next thing you know they are standing before a judge whose wondering how this ever made it to court in the first place. Case in point—don't use your plan B to threaten the other side.

Executing your Backup Plan

Remember that plan B is power. Your plan B, depending on how well you developed it is the raw power that you have. It can be used to serve your purpose or it can be used to hurt the other side. Remember that you want to execute your plan B with your rational mind doing the driving—not your emotional mind because more likely than not, your emotional mind will be thinking on how to exact revenge on your counterpart for not coming to an agreement and wasting your time. Don't abuse your power, especially if you have more of it than the other side.

Minimal force necessary. A police officer is taught in the academy how to determine the appropriate level of force to control non-complying subjects. They are taught to use the minimal amount of force necessary to gain control of the situation. This can range from verbal commands, come-along holds, up to and including lethal force. This force continuum is designed to prevent the use of excessive force out on the street. In much the same way, a negotiator who is going to use their plan B, must use the minimal amount of force necessary to convince their counterpart to return to the negotiating table. Any use of excessive force will result in a drawn out fight between parties that will be more ego-based than rational. A labor union that does not get their contract met might go on strike, but they try to keep it peaceful and discourage terrorizing customers or blocking entrances. On a national level, nations can impose shipping embargos on other nations to get them to comply without having to resort to full out war. So don't abuse your power and use the least evasive tool that gets the job done—that is bringing the other side back to the negotiating table.

Final Word

Eager to Become A Master

A martial arts student went to his teacher and said earnestly, "I am devoted to studying your martial system. How long will it take me to master it." The teacher's reply was casual, "Ten years." Impatiently, the student answered, "But I want to master it faster than that. I will work very hard. I will practice everyday, ten or more hours a day if I have to. How long will it take then?" The teacher thought for a moment, "20 years."

Learning how to defuse conflict and reach agreements is a life-long learning process. A true peace-keeper is one who does not assume that they know everything and who is willing to empty their cup when talking to every new person that they encounter so that they can learn more. Allow the world to be your greatest teacher and use every opportunity that presents itself throughout each day as a lesson to be reflected upon. Use every opportunity to listen openly without judgment and without evaluation and you will find that the world will open itself to you in your quest to become a better communicator. Best of luck to you.

Street Glossary

Active Listening: The primary skill of effective communication. Active listening involves encouraging conversation, acknowledging, paraphrasing, and showing empathy. The goal of active listening is to build trust, collect information about interests, and diffuse anger and tension.

Acknowledging: A part of active listening. It is the skill of showing your counterpart that you are internalizing and understanding everything that is said to them. It is feedback to them in the form of verbal and nonverbal communication.

Anger: A dangerous emotion that shuts down rational thought and causes reaction rather than response. It destroys one's ability to negotiate effectively.

Antisocial Personality Disorder: An abnormal personality disorder classified in the DSM-IV and characterized by the main traits of having little or no feelings of remorse, guilt, or empathy for other people. People who have APD are also known as sociopaths, psychopaths, and habitual liars.

Arbitration: A form of alternative dispute resolution where an impartial third party, typically an expert on the law, such as a judge or lawyer, hears the arguments of both parties and uses their application of existing facts and the law to award judgment on one of the two parties.

Bargaining Chips: The pieces (chips) of negotiating power that you bring to the table. These can include, but are not limited to: your plan B, knowledge, intelligence information, qualifications, competence, trust, etc.

Bartering: An exchange of goods and services without the use of money.

BATNA: Best alternative to a negotiated settlement (see Plan B)

Body Language: The gestures, poses, movements, and expressions that a person uses to communicate.

Bottom Line: This is your minimum acceptable agreement in a negotiation. Anything lower than your bottom line would be less than your plan B and therefore not worth negotiating for.

Closed-Ended Questions: Questions that you ask your counterpart that can be answered with a "yes" or a "no."

Closing: Ending the negotiation with an agreement, or by implementing your plan B.

Coding: Taking your idea and translating that idea into a tangible language that can be interpreted by another person. In face-to-face conversation, coding takes the form of verbal language, body language, and other nonverbal communication.

Conflict Resolution: The technical term for diffusing anger and hostility. Conflict resolution is achieved through active listening and reframing skills.

Concession: Something that you are willing to hand over to the other side in a negotiation.

Cooperation: One of the three underlying principles in Street Negotiation. Cooperation seeks to generate compliance from your counterpart by seeing them as a partner rather than an adversary.

Demands: a "yes or no" solid position that manifests itself out of interests. It is the cause of conflict.

Desires: The needs that accompany an unsatisfied state.

Difficult People: People who dig into positional negotiating styles or people who are thinking with their emotional mind rather than their rational mind.

Emotional Mind: Your ego-driven mind that seeks to fulfill emotional needs, by reacting rather than using logic. The emotional mind is dangerous for the negotiator because it is unpredictable and not rational.

Empathy: Seeing an issue from the perspective and mind-set of the other person. Understanding why they see things the way that they do by "walking around in their shoes." Empathy does not mean that you agree with the person or have pity on them, but rather that you understand their motivations for doing or thinking what they do.

Encouraging Conversation: Getting your counterpart to voluntarily comply with talking to you more.

Face-saving: Taking into account the other person's feelings of embarrassment and handling a situation in a way that minimizes such embarrassment.

Fair Standards: Objective criteria, benchmarks, or precedents that are used as a filter to help narrow options.

Flexibility: One of the three underlying principles to Street Negotiation. Flexibility is your ability to adapt to the infinite number of different personality types and situations that you will encounter on a daily basis. Flexibility gives you the ability to adapt to whatever situation comes your way by changing your approach and your methods of negotiation to custom fit the situation and the person you are negotiating with.

Forgiveness: The ability to let past wrongdoings go and move forward with your life. Forgiveness does not mean that you will forget the past or reconcile with the person, only that you choose to move out of the past and into the present.

Goals: Your primary objective in a negotiation.

Gossip: Destructive and inaccurate sharing of entrusted or confidential information about your personal life. Gossip destroys reputations.

Insults: Personal attacks or verbal abuse directed at you because of emotional reaction.

Integrity: Having the personal character to do the things that you say and being reliable and accountable for your actions.

Interests: Your needs and desires that lie underneath positions.

Intimidation: A negotiation strategy used by bullies who use their aggressive qualities to cloud your rational mind with fear.

Manipulate: A dirty negotiating strategy of using deceit, false-promises, and lies to satisfy your interests at the expense of the other person.

Mediation: A form of alternative dispute resolution where an objective third party is used to help both parties reach an agreement.

Mirroring: Matching your body, voice, and breathing to that of your counterpart. Mirroring places you on the same wavelength as your counterpart and makes it easier for them to trust and understand you.

Negotiating Range: The range of possible options that you would consider in satisfying your interests and needs. The best possible agreement is what you will strive for, while your bottom-line is your minimum agreement that is acceptable to you.

No-agreement alternative: The best solution you can come up with on your own without having to negotiate anything (see plan B).

Nonverbal Communication: Unspoken communication that is made up of body language, facial expressions, vocalics, and appearance that is said to account for approximately 90% of communication.

Open-ended Questions: Questions that allow your counterpart to respond with their own ideas, opinions, and suggestions.

Options: Creative ways both you and your counterpart can fulfill needs.

Paraphrasing: Part of the active listening process. It is the skill of taking someone's words and telling it back to them in the context of your own words. Paraphrasing allows you to get the correct information and avoid miscommunication as well as builds trust in the other person by showing that you are empathizing with them. This makes them an active listener themselves because they have to correct your misinterpretations.

Personal attack: Verbally abusive statements directed towards you.

Plan B: also known as your walk-away alternative, no-agreement alternative, or best alternative to a negotiated settlement (BATNA). Your plan B is the best solution that you can come up with without even having to negotiate with your counterpart. It is your main source of leverage in any type of negotiation in which you get involved.

Position: Your stance on an issue. Same as a demand.

Preparation: The steps involved before you sit down at the negotiating table. Preparation involves developing your plan B, having clearly defined goals, having a negotiating range, researching the items and people to be discussed, and knowing your interests, options, and possible solutions.

Rational Mind: Your logic-driven state of mind that focuses on achieving the best possible solution for any given situation. This is the negotiating mind-set that needs to be in control because it uses all available information and weighs all the possible options in determining a good solution.

Reaction: An emotional response to a verbal attack. The three main types of reactions are: defending, counterattacking, withdrawal.

Reframing: Taking a negative or positional statement and changing it into a statement designed to be positive or problem solving. Reframing seeks to uncover hidden interests by digging underneath the superficial and often negative statement, with the use of problem-solving questions. It is also used to move verbally abusive attacks away from you and onto the problem.

Respect: One of the three underlying principles of Street Negotiation. Respect is the ability to treat your counterpart with face-saving dignity. It generates trust and compliance. Whether the person is a doctor or a child molester, they should be given respect at the negotiation table.

Responding: Using the rational mind to effectively deal with a personal attack.

Solution: An agreement to a negotiation that is derived from mutually generated options.

Standards: also known as benchmarks, criteria, or objective standards. These are the objective 3rd party opinions that apply to your particular negotiation that help you select fair options. These can be fair market price, laws and policies, or objective views on the monetary value of time and disservice.

Street Negotiation: A way of cooperative social interaction that seeks on fulfilling mutual interests and needs. It focuses on not reaching an agreement, but rather exploring the possibility of achieving a better deal than what can be obtained without negotiation.

Stress: The feeling of anxiety you experience when all of life's demands exceed your personal resources and your ability to meet those demands.

Sympathy: Having the feeling of pity or remorse for the person. Sympathy is not and should not be confused with empathy. A Street Negotiator empathizes with the person by attempting to understand their perspective, but does not sympathize or agree with their ideas.

Tactical: A specific and efficient way of doing something or solving a problem.

Tactics: Strategies upon which objectives can be realized.

Threats: Revealing to the other side what your Plan B is. Threats are worthless because they are in the form of a direct challenge to the other person and it becomes a competition on who has the better plan B. Not only that, but by threatening, you also just gave away your plan B to the other side, so now they have more information than you do.

Translating: A process in effective communication. Translating is the ability to collect the coded signals from the other person and convert those signals into an accurate replica of the original idea.

Trust: The shared expectation that the both of you can depend on each other to achieve a common purpose.

Verbal Gifts: Specific praise that you use tactically to gain favor and generate compliance.

Verbal Self-Defense: A way of protecting yourself from negative and abusive verbal attacks, either direct or subtle, by reframing them away from you and onto the greater problem at hand.

Violence: A win/lose type of negotiation involving physical power and at least one idiot who can't control his emotions.

Win/lose negotiating: Also known as positional bargaining. A style of negotiating where each negotiator attempts to increase their position at the expense of the others.

Win/win style negotiating: Also known as principled or interest-based negotiating. A style of negotiating where each negotiator seeks to achieve a solution that is in the best interests of both parties.

References

Allen, Elizabeth L., J.D., Mohr, Donald, D., M.A., 1998. *Affordable Justice—How to settle any dispute, including divorce, out of court.* Encinitas, California. West Coast Press.

Edelman, Joel and Crain, Mary B. 1993. *The Tao of Negotiation—How You Can Prevent, Resolve, and Transcend Conflict in Work and Everyday Life.* New York: HarperCollins.

Glass, Lilian. 1999. *The Complete Idiot's Guide to Verbal Self-Defense.* Indianapolis, IN: Alpha Books.

The Harvard Business School Guide—Dealing With Difficult People. 2005. Cambridge, MA: Harvard Business School Publishing Corporation.

Hogan, Kevin. 2005. *The Science of Influence—How to Get Anyone to Say Yes in 8 Minutes or Less.* New Jersey: John Wiley & Sons, Inc.

Karrass, Gary. 1985. *Negotiate To Close.* New York, New York. Simon and Schuster, Inc.

Levinson, Jay C., Smith, Mark S., Wilson, Orvel R. 1999. *Guerrilla Negotiating—Unconventional Weapons and Tactics to Get What You Want.* New York: John Wiley & Sons, Inc.

Lum, Grande. 2005. *The Negotiation Fieldbook.* New York: McGraw-Hill

Misino, Dominick J. and Defelice, Jim. 2004. *Negotiate and Win—Proven Strategies from the NYPD's Top Hostage Negotiator.* New York: McGraw Hill.

Quilliam, Susan. 1997. *Body Language Secrets.* Hammersmith, London. HarperCollins Publishing.

Pease, Allan. 1981. *Signals: How to Use Body Language for Power, Success, and Love.* New York, New York: Bantam Books

Pinet, Angelique. 2005. *The Everything Negotiating Book.* Avon, MA: F+W Publications.

Stark, Peter B. and Flaherty, Jane. 2003. *The Only Negotiating Guide You'll Ever Need.* New York: Broadway Books.

Ury, William. 1993. *Getting Past No—Negotiating Your Way From*

Confrontation to Cooperation. New York: Bantam Books.

Wainwright, Gordon R. 2003. *Body Language.* Chicago, Illinois. McGraw-Hill Companies.

About The Author

Tristan J. Loo is the founder and Chief Executive of Alternative Conflict Resolution Services, a training/consulting/mediation firm based out of San Diego County, California. Mr. Loo is a former police officer, conflict intervention consultant, professional mediator, certified negotiator, Tactical Conflict Resolution™ trainer, and prolific writer/author of numerous conflict publications. While other conflict *"experts"* were spending their time learning from books and lectures, Mr. Loo was actively engaging conflict out on the streets, honing his knowledge and understanding of conflict during hundreds of dangerous encounters with hostile and violent subjects. Mr. Loo's experience handling extreme situations of conflict gave him a unique perspective into the dynamics of conflict resolution, which cannot be taught by any conventional institution. A peacekeeper at heart, Mr. Loo strongly believes that by separating the people and their emotions from the problem, conflict can be made into a constructive and positive experience for growth.

Mr. Loo likens the societal problem of conflict mishandling to the old Zen teaching of removing a fly from a friend's face by taking his head off with a hatchet. "Conflict resolution is easy. We all know how to resolve conflict. The problem is that we often select the hatchet to remove the fly when a gentle puff of air would accomplish the same thing. I created ACRS to help people solve problems without having to reach for the hatchet."

Mr. Loo's motto is, "To overcome without attacking. To defend without resisting. To control without forcing. To win without fighting."

About Alternative Conflict Resolution Services

Alternative Conflict Resolution Services (ACRS) provides conflict training, coaching, and resolution services to individuals and organizations interested in finding more effective and proactive ways to deal with conflict. Our goal is to empower people through non-adversarial means to solve problems, build and preserve relationships, reduce violence, and promote constructive growth. Our motto is, "Winning wars without fighting battles."

Our Services:

Tactical Conflict Resolution Training. Tactical Conflict Resolution is a practical system of peacemaking designed for people who need the tools to defuse hostile people and reach agreements in either their professional or personal lives. TCR focuses on reframing negative adversarial behavior into cooperative problem-solving by first dealing with the underlying needs and emotions involved and then building a bridge towards mutual agreement that both parties can live with. With workplace violence, hostile customers, and litigation on the rise; TCR is your main line of defense.

Conflict Coaching. We provide private one-on-one conflict coaching for individuals who would like help and support to overcome and resolve conflict in their professional or personal lives. Conflict coaching is a confidential process that blends the fields of conflict resolution and coaching together into one comprehensive package designed to help individuals develop constructive and progressive ways of dealing with workplace or personal conflict situations. Conflict is both inevitable and unavoidable in life and it can be either constructive or destructive to you and those around you, depending on the way it is handled. Our collaborative approach to coaching will enable you to tackle the most difficult conflict situations and turn it into a positive chance for personal growth.

Dispute Mediation Services. Mediation is the assisted negotiation between two parties in conflict with the aid of a neutral third-party. The mediator does not decide the outcome of the dispute, rather it's the mediator's job to control the process of the conflict as well as the emotions involved so that mutually-beneficial solutions can be developed between the disputing parties. We offer professional mediation services to individuals and organizations that have a dispute and are willing to try mediation as a form of alternative dispute resolution. Mediation is the safe and logical choice for most individuals before a costly legal battle is engaged.

Books & Learning Products. ACRS publishes a variety of books, workbooks, and training materials on conflict related areas. Check out our website for new titles. ACRS publishes our own proprietary quick reference cards designed for people who don't have time to study or people who need to look up important information fast. A Quick-Card is a learning product with our expert information categorized, color-coded, and sorted for easy reference. We specialize in developing learning cards in the areas of conflict resolution, conflict management, effective communication, self-improvement, and business skills. QuickCards make the ideal reference guide to carry along with you wherever you go.

To learn more, visit the ACRS website at:
www.acrsonline.com
or send email to:
info@acrsonline.com

Inquiries and requests can also be sent to:

Alternative Conflict Resolution Services
306-N West El Norte Parkway #317
Escondido, CA 92026
Fax (760) 466-7564

Street Negotiation
Order Form

- **Website (fastest & preferred method).** Secure online ordering through our website at www.acrsonline.com
- **Fax.** (760) 466-7564 (fax this form)
- **Mail.** We accept check, money order, or credit card. Mail this form to: ACRS, 306-N West El Norte Parkway #317, Escondido, CA 92026

Please send_____copies of *Street Negotiation*

Company_____

Name_____

Shipping Address_____

City_____State_____Zip_____

Telephone _____Fax_____

E-Mail _____

Price: $24.95 (subject to change)
Shipping/Handling. $3.50/book within the U.S. $6.00 to Canada. Contact us for group discounts and for shipping rates to other countries.

Payment amount: Quantity____ x $24.95 = $ _____
Sales tax 7.75% ($1.93/book) Ca residents only..... $ _____
                    Shipping.................. $ _____
                    Total......................... $ _____

Check_____Credit____ ____Money Order_____
Card Type (circle one) Visa/MasterCard/Amex/Discover
Credit Card # _____Exp. Date___/20____
Card Verification # (3-digit # located on back of card)_____ _____
First Name_____
Last Name_____
Billing address (for credit card)_____
City_____State_____Zip_____

Signature_____

• • •

Printed in the United States
110519LV00004B/351/A